PAUL CARELL • OPERATION BARBAROSSA IN PHOTOGRAPHS

PAUL CARELL

OPERATION BARBAROSSA IN PHOTOGRAPHS

THE WAR IN RUSSIA
AS PHOTOGRAPHED BY THE SOLDIERS

With a New Preface by the Author

Translated from the German by William Warda Sr.

Schiffer Military/Aviation History
Atglen, PA

Translated from the German by William Warda, Sr.
Proofreading by William Warda, Jr.

Note: The references in the text to Mr. Carell's works, *Operation Barbarossa* and *Scorched Earth*, are to the German language editions published by Verlag Ullstein as, *Unternehmen Barbarossa* (*Operation Barbarossa*, also known as *Hilter Moves East*) and *Verbrannte Erde* (*Scorched Earth*).

Copyright © 1991 by Schiffer Publishing Ltd..
Library of Congress Catalog Number: 90-62986

Printed in China
ISBN: 0-88740-280-1
We are interested in hearing from authors with book ideas on related topics.

This book originally published under the title,
Unternehmen Barbarossa im Bild,
by Verlag Ullstein GmbH, Berlin-Frankfurt/M.,
© 1985. ISBN: 3-550-08509-5.

Published by Schiffer Publishing Ltd.
4880 Lower Valley Road
Atglen, PA 19310
Phone: (610) 593-1777
FAX: (610) 593-2002
E-mail: Schifferbk@aol.com.
Please write for a free catalog.
This book may be purchased from the publisher.
Please include $3.95 postage.
Try your bookstore first.

CONTENTS

The list below gives the equivalent wartime ranks of the Waffen-SS, the Wehrmacht and the U.S. Army

Waffen-SS	Wehrmacht	U.S. Army
General Officers		
- No equivalent -	Generalfeldmarschall	General of the Army
Oberstgruppenführer	Generaloberst	General
Obergruppenführer	General	Lieutenant General
Gruppenführer	Generalleutnant	Major General
Brigadeführer	Generalmajor	Brigadier General
Staff Officers		
Oberführer	- No Equivalent -	- No Equivalent -
(*Wore the shoulder strap of a Colonel*)		
Standartenführer	Oberst	Colonel
Obersturmführer	Oberstleutnant	Lieutenant Colonel
Sturmbannführer	Major	Major
Company Officers		
Hauptsturmführer	Hauptmann	Captain
Obersturmführer	Oberleutnant	1st Lieutenant
Untersturmführer	Leutnant	2nd Lieutenant
Officer Candidates (*Basically equal to Oberfeldwebel & Feldwebel*)		
Oberjunker	Oberfähnrich	- No Equivalent -
Junker	Fähnrich	- No Equivalent -
Non-commissioned Officers		
Sturmscharführer	Stabsfeldwebel	Sergeant Major
Hauptscharführer	Oberfeldwebel	Master Sergeant
Oberscharführer	Feldwebel	Technical Sergeant
Scharführer	Unterfeldwebel	Staff Sergeant
Unterscharführer	Unteroffizier	Sergeant
Enlisted Men		
- No Equivalent -	Stabagefreiter	Admin. Corporal
Rottenführer	Obergefreiter	Corporal
Sturmmann	Gefreiter	Corporal
SS-Obersoldat*	Obersoldat*	Private 1st Class
SS-Soldat*	Soldat*	Private

---

*Note: Soldat is a general term. Other words here are Schütz, Grenadier, Füsilier, depending upon the combat arm to which the soldier belonged.

Source of U.S. World War II army equivalents: War Department Technical Manual TM-E 30-451, *Handbook on German Military Forces*, 15 March 1945.

PREFACE

*T*he photographs in this volume tell everything about war, about every war — not only the German-Russian. After more than four decades, the actual drama of the snapshot is not essential any more; it is the sign of bravery or fear, acting or suffering, ordering or obeying — but removed from time, and turning into a document, where the photo becomes truth.

Truth is more than reality. Especially on account of this, every picture documenting place and time, is set in the military context.

Of importance for the non-German viewer: photos taken by soldiers during a war reveal extreme situations of life. Death is the godfather of every picture; shining through the military's every day humdrum, the triviality of life photographed in war. Eating, drinking, entertainment and fun, relaxing or training — still close to death.

The prime example for soldierly virtue is expressed in the German word "Kamerad" — the indispensible sister of misery. Maybe comradeship is the only true virtue of war. She glows in every theatre of war for every soldier of any army.

What I tried to achieve with these photos — shot by German and Russian soldiers, without any tendentious purpose — was to make the presentation more realistic. This picture volume does not carry any nationalistic overtones, it is simply pictures of soldiers, regardless of uniform or war theatre — Fritz or Tommy, GI or Ivan.

Paul Carell   Hamburg, September 1990

INTRODUCTION

"*M*oschaisk in German hands" must have been the most shattering news of the war for Moscow. This report from the historic battlefield of Borodino seemed to seal the fate of the Capital in October 1941 the same way as in September 1812, after Napoleon broke through the entrenchments of Rajekski. Writing the history of the bloody encounters between the 40th Panzerkorps and the tough fighters of the 32nd Siberian Rifle-division, I received a series of photos of the battles and the surrounding landscape of Moschaisk. Now I stood on the same heights overlooking the city. To the east along the highway of Moschaisk, the view travels far towards Moscow. The truth of military intelligence reports comes in a flash to you: Possessing these heights, your foot is in the doorstep of Moscow.

There I recognized the power of a photo, deepening the understanding of events and happenings, which are difficult to comprehend and almost impossible to visualize for any reader. General Fritz Bayerlein, Rommel's chief of General staff, and an experienced divisional commander confirmed more than once: "An instructive photo is worth more than a twenty page description of some terrain."

Imagine the vastness of the steppes — a sea of flowers and grasses in the relentless heat of the summer; an ocean of snow in winter — to fathom the fatigue of the marching and fighting. You have to see the wide Russian streams to understand what it meant to cross them without loss of time; the endless columns of prisoners marching to the west after being surrounded; the catastrophe that befell the Russians becomes visible on the Steppes when they were beaten during the first half of the year 1941. The impact of the winter photos of 1941/42: demonstrating without pity the freeze of Hitler's Blitzkrieg; General Winter beating the paralyzed German Armies in front of Moscow. A new summer came. A new winter. The pictures explain. They show the gulches of the wooded Caucasus, the glaciers of Elbrus mountains. The Don. The Volga. The Terek. The treeless steppes. Primeval forests of the Volkhov. The icy chill of the Neva and frozen Lake Ilmen. Once more they show the elementary obstacles of endless tracts, limiting the greatest bravery and preventing the last steps to a decisive goal; regardless if the name was Murmansk or Moscow, Tuapse or Tiflis, Astrakhan or Stalingrad.

Observing the steep bank of the Volga, the term "our Wonder Weapon" used by the Red Army, leaves no doubt in anyone's mind that every step was to be paid in blood, is fully understandable, viewing the chaos of Stalingrad's factory buildings; or the icy landscapes in the central sector, showing yard-high snow drifts stopping trucks and Panzer alike. Photos become irrevocable witnesses of the murderous winter battles, separating the Kremlin from the German infantry by only sixteen Kilometers and saving Moscow.

Holding a photo of a military column on its way to Stalingrad that first summer, an amazed young coworker asked: "Did anyone ever ask what would happen if winter came and dumped up to three meters of snow there?" Yes, but nobody ever thought much about it. The same question turns up, looking at pictures of mud mired main roads which practically drowned divisions with horses and carts during the Spring "Rasputiza" (thaw) or the Fall morasses. Was this ever considered? Here the photo becomes the unquestionable exclamation mark of any critique at this point. There are pictures of a simple gesture — the ordering index finger of an officer, a frozen stiff hand of a dead soldier removed from time; deeply emotional pictures depicting humanity; evidence of gripping bravery and bitter despair of a child behind the front lines. These pictures tell everything about war, not only the German-Russian war but every war. The character of the snapshot, its actual dramatics faded after two decades, leaving a sign, a symbol of courage or rage, fear or melancholy, dealing with a situation or suffering. Still a painting of the spiritual landscape, a timeless impression pointing out and awakening basic emotions. Scanning these photos summons hate or love, sadness or anger. One tiny piece of reality caught by the snapshot of a soldier, becomes evidence of the whole truth. But be aware: Truth is more than reality. The fact justifies the symbolic photo, representing the truth which exceeds reality.

Point in case; the photo on page 123: Excellently equipped Siberians in winter outfits, marching past dead Germans in their summer coats, frozen rigid in the ditches. There it is the Siberian ace in the hole for the bloody gamble for Moscow, out in the open. From the military point of view, a small unimportant scene becomes a star witness for a very important fact.

FORM AND IDEA BEHIND THIS VOLUME

It is very difficult to wade through a stream of four- or five hundred pages of pictures. A photo and a caption. Photo. Caption. And so on and on. Page after page. I tried to escape the monotony, by giving each double-page a theme. The flow of pictures turns thus into bulwarks and islands. Graphic signs, vignettes, sketches of maps and abrupt changes of themes should be of help to the viewer. "The Cigarette", being a double-page in the middle of the complex summer and fall battles of 1941, is no coincidence. Neither are the four double-pages of front line theatre, found during the fighting for the Kursk salient. I don't know if all viewers will accept it, but it is my opinion that even a picture volume of war and soldiers has the right to some artful stratagems. Some double-pages are supposed to imitate a movie, creating something alive and contemporary. Like the motorcycle troop enterprise or the infantry storming, one phase as close as possible to the other. Soldiers marching, looking over to a window with young girls. There is no use of setups or falsified order of picture sequences. Photos taken from a different sector, a different timetable are marked; but only to emphasize a certain fact. I tried to use a picture as a true source where, when and — if necessary — how it was taken. A photo can also be very deceptive. Failing to study the source, it is easy to be duped; if a scene was faked or genuine; if time and place were given correctly; if the original caption was used for a special purpose and why.

Until today the "Photo alibi", with falsified inscriptions is constantly in use. We tried to avoid anything that was questionable. Did we succeed? The idea of presenting our readers with this manifold, documentary picture material, grew out of the research for *Operation Barbarossa*; evaluating photos for their impact in battle situations, certain moods, and the places of events. The many reasons not to employ as many pictures as text, created the idea of a fully illustrated volume. A pictorial volume in which the photo in its many functions stands side by side with the reports of the text book. From this day on we started collecting. Always searching for the best examples, not beautiful or big or even faultless photos. Poor picture quality to emphasize certain sectors, a central point or to underscore an event in my books, was often accepted by us. For example: The bridge over the Terek by Mozdok;

overlooking the Neva at Porogi; landscape around the infamous Poseloks near Schlüsselburg. Two photos of the battle for Moscow:one German, the other Russian, are absolute models. Side by side they hold a unique, eerie power not given to any other media: "Fall in" — "Killed"!

Another way of choosing our pictures: The encirclement at Cherkassy at the beginning of 1944; tragedy between the Dnieper and Gniloy Tikich. Hard hitting pictures showing action, battle and retreat from the cauldron. Horrible photos of the ice covered Gniloy Tikich are not in existence; who should have taken them? Running and swimming for your life is hardly the situation to take snapshots!

The question was: How to fill a double-page, having only one picture for the theme Cherkassy? It had to be an uncommon portrayal of a fighting scene. This encirclement was more than just a military disaster. First of all, it was human tragedy, particularly for those thinking they were saved; they raced straight into the arms of death. I chose a very unpathetic picture: The last meal — a guaranteed, documented photo of the hour of retreat. The Russian photo, based on proudly gathered information, of a legitimate war report provide: a shocking contrast — the conquered battleground.

These two photos, visible supports in bridging the imperceptible towards the tragedy described in *Scorched Earth*.

Choosing photos for the composition of the volume, these examples point distinctly in the direction of our thoughts. They also answer the questions of my friends; why this snapshot was used and not the one I gave you? Sometimes the choice was extremely difficult. Stay with the fundamental idea: despite the plentiful variety, keep the volume unified — one picture of many! *Operation Barbarossa* and *Scorched Earth* demonstrated the theme of the military and soldiers' drama during the war in Russia. It is not my job to exhibit guilt, but to keep history alive. My search is for truth, not folly. Truth being manifested to the fighter in his various forms, while he took his pictures of his own war experience. Photographed by a soldier — captions are limited. Where are the pictures of the concentration camps? The gas chambers? Never being objects relating to the soldier and the front, they don't have a place in my books. An entirely different fact are the rear areas of the front lines, the occupied zones, exposed to an ever increasing development of force and counterforce, namely, the inhuman war of partisans demanding victims. Few photos exist of certain operations. Chaotic developments, break-outs of encirclements, hasty retreats do not allow a change from gun to camera. *Nothing* was more important than survival.

It is impossible to have documented photos for every sector, assault or other momentous events entailed in my writings, not because there are no pictures: economic considerations allowing, a low price for a wide readership is a must, and the extent of a given volume, restrict almost all writing. One photo has to represent a full sector. Example: Cholm; Kharkov; the Hube cauldron; Finnish troops marching on a mountain road; the group from Jäger-regiment 139; all of them represent the fighting for Murmansk.

The appalling picture of the wounded from the II. Batallion, 26th Infantry Regiment stands for all the misery of battle (Page 432). This small, 6 x 9 cm photo was taken by Jakob Moll in the summer of 1941; finding it in an album, it seemed tiny, insignificant, but later magnification displayed a breath-taking document one of the most impressive photos. One additional page for "Repairs", the medics, railroad personnel, engineers, would have been fully justified. Special themes demanded preference — my feeble excuse. One question surely will be raised: why do so many pictures have precise, documentary descriptions — unit, time, name of photographer, perfect wording — others only a few vague words? There is a purpose behind it! Symbolic use of a picture rejects everything, even details or information in favor of the truth.

An overriding motive from the first to the last page: the face of the fighter! Both, German and Russian. Passing years changed not only his face, but everything else about him. His eyes, the bearing, his battle dress and manners. Reflecting not only the actual fighting, but also the boring phases of war. Any given photo of a gun firing, an assault group, a single marksman, reveals time and change of the soldiers' story. German conquerors turn losers, beaten Red troops mature into tough victors. Above all, the photos show startling resemblances in the soldiers faces, despite every transformation. This becomes very visible considering the fact that war is not only shooting, driving, winning, dying and losing, but eating and drinking, sewing and nailing, bandaging and operating, healing and burying, being supplied, repaired and trained. Bureaucracy flowered behind the front lines; there was love and hate, kindness and horror. All this belonged into the curious and unique world of the soldier, claiming more than 90% of it.

Something else: the land on which war raged, was a temporary battleground, and still, people partially occupied it, and even soldiers lived with them in their houses and huts! They bartered and traded; and winter still found them at their stoves.

Particular for this chapter the scenery of war, color photos play an essential part. They form the unusual documents. There are no comparable photos of one of the former enemy countries available, in particular of Russia and only very few of the Pacific war or the Far Eastern fronts. The forties saw color photography taking its first steps. German soldiers making it a hobby always had special connections to the big German photo companies. These in turn provided the rare films and took care in developing them. This explains these unprecedented photos.

GUIDE FOR THE VIEWER

Everytime my co-workers and myself viewed pictorial volumes the same thing happened. At first your interest is very high, you look and study; then you only look and pretty soon you are only turning pages. Reading is much less tiresome than concentric viewing. To offer more reading material, the subtitles had to be more descriptive. So, you loose room and white space necessary for the frame and aesthetic decor. More text would stimulate reading, but also destroy the basic impact of a picture; the picture book becomes a reading book with pictures. We strove for the opposite.

I'm not the first facing this problem — there are different ways to overcome this obstruction. One could present information and explanation in a separate supplement; exchanging text and picture pages another possibility; arranging text in the form of a document, the camouflage trick, is a way out. My decision was to use a different approach — to stay within the laws of graphic documents, maps and diagrams have to be sparse. I stayed with the primary power of the photo. Detailed descriptions appear in *Operation Barbarossa* and *Scorched Earth*. Part I. corresponds with the chapter "Moscow" of *Operation Barbarossa*.

Part II. "At Moscow's Doorsteps" finds its parallels in the chapters "Moscow" in *Operation Barbarossa*.

Part III. "Storm at the Southern Wing" explained in the chapters "Rostov", "Caucasus and the Oil" of *Operation Barbarossa*.

Part IV. "Stalingrad", identical name for the chapter in *Operation Barbarossa*.

Part V. "The Battles of the Northern Wing", reflected in the chapters "Leningrad", "Winter Battle", and "Harbors on the Arctic Sea" of *Operation Barbarossa* as well as in the chapter "The Battles of the Northern Wing" of *Scorched Earth*.

Part VI. "Caucasus, Kuban, Kerch" are the chapter "Caucasus and the Oil" in *Operation Barbarossa*, and, chapter "Manstein" of *Scorched Earth*.

Part VII. "Operation Citadel" corresponds with chapter "Battle for Kursk" in *Scorched Earth*.

Part VIII. "Scorched Earth" is portrayed in the chapters "To the Dneiper" and "Between Kiev and Melitopol" of *Scorched Earth*.

Part IX. Finally "The Front Collapses" depicted in the chapters "Between Kiev and Melitopol", "Chaos on the Southern Wing", "Army Group Center's Cannae" from *Scorched Earth*.

The illustrated volume, without breaking its restrictions, can thus be made into a reading book; separated by a glance, reader turns into viewer. Special help for the military historian is provided on pages 23-29 presenting a chronological sequence of events. The battle calendar adheres to the chapters of the picture volume.

Thanks to my co-workers

Thanking those who helped the author is a most pleasant part of any book. None of my books would have been written without the help of my co-workers, helpers, informants and advisers. I am in their debt. To name all of them is nearly impossible.

Photographers and owners of furnished photos are represented in the source of pictures. Most of the time a repeated name as "source" is also a sign for years of fruitful, companionable co-operation. In particular Georg Brütting, Professor Determeyer, Andres Feldle, Walter Hackl, Carl Henrich, Walter Holters, Hanns-Ritter Klippert, Hans Klöckner, Herbert Kuntz, Friedrich Musculus, Fritz Niederlein, Dr. Alfred Ott, Ernst-A. Paulus, Professor Dr. Priesack, Franz Regnery, Asmus Remmer, Horst Scheibert, Dr. med. vet. Hermann Schmidt, Karl Schwoon, Heinz Sellhorn, Otto Tenning, Emil Thrän, Gerhard Tietz, Gottfried Tornau, Hans-Joachim Tripp and Dr. Kurt Winterfeld.

A very special thanks to the Soviet Embassy in Bonn and the Novosti Agency of Moscow, allowing us to use over 400 well lettered, valuable documentary photos of all phases of the war.

A few, but well deserved words of thanks have to go to Bernhard Ziegler, an exceptional craftsman, solving the graphic problems with empathy, which only an artist and former Landser, as himself, could do. Assorting 20,000 photos, choosing the most striking, arranging them in proper sequence, proved not only to be a vexing, but also a time consuming task. Thanks are due to my co-worker Heinz Westphal for his untiring perseverance by providing the documents for the insignias of the divisions. Despite grave doubts by the editors, the final result was outstanding. Published to such an extent for the first time, these symbols may remind some who forgot the tactical sign of their division. The painstaking work of documentation, which makes or breaks a work of this kind, deserve special thanks to Herr Günter Wegmann. Thanks to Herr *Oberstleutnant* Rolf Stoves for reviewing the manuscript, and Herrn Oberst a.D. Boje for the careful revision of the battle calendar. What would have happened — or not — if the hand over the author and co-workers named by a *Generaloberst* , "Chief of Staff", and known to all of us, was not evident?

Everyone including author, co-workers and advisers agree: thanks belong to the large community of Carell readers, giving strength and courage for the backbreaking, exhausting labor demanded by the preparation of this non-fiction and picture volume.

Hamburg, October 1967   PAUL CARELL

Chronology

CHRONOLOGICAL LISTING OF EASTERN FRONT OPERATIONS

I. BLITZKRIEG AND ENCIRCLEMENTS

6/22-6/28/41	Breaking through border fortifications on the Bug and conquest of Brest-Litowsk
6/22-6/25/41	Breaking through border fortifications in Lithuania
6/22-7/7/41	Breaking through border fortifications in Galicia and West Ukraine
6/23-6/28/41	Fighting in the Pripjet swamp region
6/24/41	Kovno falls
6/26-6/29/41	Battle for Dünaburg
6/28/41	Bobruysk reached
6/28-6/30/41	Battle for Lemberg
6/29/41	Libau taken
6/29-7/1/41	Riga falls
6/29-7/12/41	Fighting in the region of Riga
6/29-7/7/41	Encirclement fighting Bialystok-Minsk
7/2-7/10/41	Battle for Tarnopol
7/2-7/25/41	Stalin line broken (Army Group South)
7/8/41	Pleskau taken
7/8-7/10/41	Vitebsk falls
7/8-7/15/41	Stalin line broken (Army Group Center)
7/8-7/14/41	Pursuit to Lake Ilmen
7/9-7/14/41	Dnieper positions broken
7/11-8/4/41	Battle for Dorpat
7/11-8/5/41	Battle for Smolensk
7/13-9/25/41	Advance and fighting in Leningrad territory
7/20-7/28/41	Fighting around Mogilev
7/25-8/8/41	Uman surrounded
8/1-8/9/41	Encirclement of Roslawl
8/9-8/20/41	Battle of Gomel
8/10-8/24/41	Battle for Staraya Russa
8/20-8/28/41	Fighting for Reval
8/22/41	Cherkassy taken
8/22-8/27/41	Battle of Velikiye-Luki
8/25/41	Panzer Group 2 (Guderian) attacking south is being turned around into rear of Budjenny
8/21-9/27/41	Encirclement of Kiev
8/31-9/30/41	Advance to the Crimea and break-through at Perekop
8/7-8/9/41	Western settlements of workers (Poseloks) at Schlüsselburg taken
9/8/41	Schlüsselburg falls
9/13-10/5/41	Bypassing Poltava
9/8-10/21/41	Baltic islands taken
9/24-9/29/41	Fighting for Dnepropetrovsk
9/26-10/11/41	Battle at the Sea of Asov
10/17-10/25/41	Fighting at Kharkov-Belgorod
10/2-10/20/41	Double-battle Vyazma-Bryansk

10/4/41	Assault on Moscow begins
10/4/41	Push for Tula
10/8-10/17/41	Fighting at Gschatsk
10/24-11/3/41	Kursk taken
10/16-12/7/41	Battling for Tikhvin
10/18/41	Crimea battle begins
11/17-11/21/41	Advance to Rostov and fall of the city

II. AT MOSCOW'S DOOR STEPS

10/12/41	Kaluga taken
10/14/41	Kalinin falls
10/19/41	Meschaisk taken
10/25/41	Gorki taken
Oct-Nov/41	Fighting for the heights of Schelkovkand Dorochovo
11/15-11/19/41	Begin of assault by Army Group Center
11/26/41	Istra falls
12/1-12/4/41	Nara positions broken, fighting for Juschkowo and Burzevo
12/5/41	Advance units 8 Kilometers before Moscow
12/6/41	Guderian stops attack for Tula
12/6-12/21/41	Beginning of a of 1,000 Kilometer wide defensive battle from Ostaschkow to Jelez
12/6-12/19/41	Defensive fighting for Klin
12/15-12/24/41	Defensive fighting between Kalinin and the winter position
December 41	Collection of winter clothing in Germany
12/19/41	*Feldmarschall* von Brauchitsch removed
12/25/41	*Generaloberst* Guderian relieved
12/21-12/30/41	Defending Kaluga
1/4-2/20/42	Winter battle of Rzhev
1/14-4/18/42	Defending the winter fortifications Juchnov-Gschatsk-Subzow
3/22-4/18/42	Battles at Vyazma

III. STORM ON THE SOUTHERN WING

	Prelude to "Operation Blue"
8/24-9/1/41	Fall of Berislav and fording the Dneiper
10/17/41	Taking Taganrog
10/20/41	Fall of Stalino
Nov 41-March 42	Winter battles in the regions Rostov-Kharkov-Kursk-Orel
11/19-11/21/41	Taking possession of Rostov and the bridges over the Don
11/29/41	Russian counter attack, Rostow evacuated
12/1/41	*Feldmarschall* von Rundstedt replaced by *Feldmarschall* von Reichenau
5/17-5/27/42	Barvenkovo (Timoschenko) surrounded
5/22-5/27/42	Encirclement battle south-west of Kharkov
6/22-6/26/42	Battle of Izyum-Kupyansk 11th Army (Manstein) conquers the Crimea
8/31-9/30/41	Breakthrough at Perekop
10/18-10/27/41	Breakthrough at Ischun
10/28-11/16/41	Breakthrough at Kerch
12/28-1/18/42	Fighting for Feodosia
5/8-5/21/42	Kerch taken
6/2-7/4/42	Sevastopol stormed. Begin "Operation Blue"
6/28-7/4/42	Battle of Voronezh
7/9-7/24/42	Breakthrough and pursuit in the Donets basin

7/20-8/13/42	Pursuit over the Lower Don
7/21-7/25/42	Rostov taken in street fighting and grabbing the large bridge of Bataisk
July-Sept/42	Push of Army Group A from Rostov over Donets, Kuban, Manych in direction of Noworossisk-Krasnodar-Pyatigorsk-Elbrus and over the Terek towards Mozdok
8/9/42	Maikop taken
8/13/42	Krasnodar falls
9/10/42	Novorossisk and Taman peninsula taken
8/18-11/18/42	Fighting in the Caucasus mountains, Mozdok-Pyatigorsk-Elbrus
8/19-12/30/42	Defensive battles in the Terek region
9/16/42	16th I.D. (mot.) scouting party stands east of Elista in immediate vicinity of Astrachan
12/31-1/28/43	Disengagement to the Lower Don
1/5-2/11/43	Disengagement to the Lower Kuban
2/12-3/31/43	Defensive battles of Kuban bridgehead; Advance of 6th Army toward Stalingrad
7/20-8/16/42	Encirclement battle in vicinity of Kalatch
8/23/42	16th Panzer Division (Hube) advances to the Volga

IV. STALINGRAD

Prelude to Stalingrad

January-April 42	Battle in the bend of Izyum south-west of Kharkov (Balakleya-Slawiansk)
5/18-5/22/42	3rd Panzerkorps (von Mackensen) surrounds Russian forces at Voltschansk north of Kharkov, and at Kupyansk
6/28/42	6th Army begins "Operation Blue" in the Kharkov area
7/4/42	Rossosch taken
7/13/42	*Feldmarschall* von Bock (Army Group B) replaced by *Generaloberst* von Weichs
7/13/42	Hitler turns 4th Panzer Army to the south
Middle July 42	11th Army (Manstein) en route to Leningrad
End of July 42	Attempts of encirclements at Stary Oskol and Millerovo unsuccessful; Timoschenko dodges in direction Stalingrad. 6th Army advances towards Stalingrad. Assault on Stalingrad
8/23/42	16th Panzer division reaches the Volga
8/31/42	4th Panzer army (Hoth) attacks city from the south-east
9/7/42	51st Army corps (von Seydlitz) advances to airport Gumrak
9/2/42	Yeremenko eludes threatening encirclement by retreating to city limits. General Lopatin ready to surrender; replaced by General Chuykov
9/14-11/19/42	Violent fighting in the city for Mamai Kurgan (Heighth 102) - grain elevator -bread factory - the "Racket" - tractor factory - smelting works "Red October" -gun manufactory "Red Barricade"
9/15-10/3/42	Six divisions of the last reserves arrive to support Yeremenko
9/16/42	General Rodimtzev's 13th Gardeschützen division, reinforcement destroyed while ferried over the Volga
11/19/42	Counter offensive of the Russians out of Kletskaya-Blinow area. Rumanian positions smashed
1/20/42	Russian counter offense out of Beketovka-Krasnoarmaisk area breaks through Rumanian defenses 29th I.D. (mot.) (General Leyser) prevents Russian breakthrough north of Sety
11/22-11/23/42	Russian advance and surprise attack take the Don heights and bridge at Kalatsch
11/22-11/23/42	6th Army surrounded
11/27/42	*Feldmarschall* von Manstein takes command of Army group Don
12/12/42	Army group Hoth starts relief attack from south
12/20/42	11th Panzerregiment (von Hünersdorff) takes Myschkowa sector about 60

	Kilometers before Stalingrad
12/23/42	6th Panzer division has to be turned away because Russian breakthrough at Morosovskaya
12/24/42	Hoth has to abandon relief attack
1/14/43	Russians take airport of Pitomnik
2/2/43	The rest of 6th Army capitulates

V. THE BATTLES ON THE NORTHERN WING

6/22/41	Army group North starts attacks between Suwalki and Memel
6/22-6/24/41	Crossing the Nyemen and fall of Kovno
6/22-6/25/41	Breaking through border fortifications in Lithuania
6/22-9/19/41	"Operation Platinum Fox" mountain corps Dietl advances towards Murmansk
6/24-6/26/41	Panzer battle on the Dubysa (1st and 6th Panzer Div.)
6/24-6/28/41	Libau taken in street fighting
6/26-6/29/41	Fall of Dünaburg
6/29-7/1/41	Riga taken
6/29-7/12/41	Fighting between Düna and Velikaye; Ostrow taken
7/1-10/14/41	Advance of 36th Army corps towards Kandalakscha
7/7/41	Pleskau taken
7/2-7/5/41	Breaking through former Latvia-Russia border fortifications
7/11-8/4/41	Battle for Dorpat
7/8-8/9/41	Breaking through Stalin-line to Lake Ilmen
8/15-8/23/41	Battle at Staraya Russia. 56th Panzer corps (Manstein) saves 10th Army corps by destroying 34th Russian Army
7/14/41	Forcing the Luga at Sabsk and Poretschye
8/16/41	Fall of Novgorod
9/2/41	Elimination of the Luga cauldron
9/8/41	Assault on Leningrad begins September 41 Oranienbaum surrounded
9/11/41	2nd defense line of Leningrad broken
9/8/41	Schlüsselburg taken
9/12/41	Assault on Leningrad stopped. City is beseiged
11/8/41	Tikhvin taken
12/8/41	Tikhvin given up. Evasive action over the Volkov
1/13-1/20/42	Start of Russian offensive over the Volkov/Breaking through German 126th and 215th I.D. (Bottleneck)
3/19/42	Mainforce of 2nd Russian assault army cut off on the Erika firebreak
2/8/42	Demyansk cauldron
From 1/23/42	Cholm cauldron
3/21/42	General Vlassov takes over leadership in the Volkov cauldron
3/21/42	"Operation Brückenschlag"
4/21/42	Liberation of Demjansk cauldron
5/5/42	Cholm cauldron relieved
End of May until 6/26/42	Annihilation of the Russian Army in the Wolchow cauldron

VI. CAUCASUS, KUBAN, KERCH

5/16/42	Kerch taken
7/1/42	Sevastopol falls
7/21-7/25/42	Rostov retaken/Bridge of Bataisk gained
8/23/42	Hitler relocates 11th Army (Manstein) to Leningrad

7/20/42	Fording the southern Don, bridgehead of Nikolewskaya
7/23/42	River Sal crossed
7/28/42	Panzer battle at Martinovka
Begin of Aug/42	Advance over the Donets, Don, Manytsch through the steppes in direction of the Caucasus
7/31/42	Dalsk taken
8/3/42	Taking Voroschilovsk
8/13/42	Crossing the Kuban and fall of Krasnodar
8/9/42	Storming the oil city of Maykop
8/12/42	Elista in the Kalmyk Steppe taken
8/21/42	Raising of the flag on Mount Elbrus
8/25/42	Mozdok falls after street fighting
9/10/42	Novorossisk taken
9/16/42	Reconnaissance units of the 16th I.D. (mot.) in very close proximity of Astrakhan (Sadovska-Senseli)
8/30/42	Crossing the Terek at Ischerskaja
9/1-2/42	and also Mozdok
From 10/25/42	Push for Ordschonikidse and Groznyy oil fields
Middle Nov/42	Caucasus front turns static
December 42	Russian attacks on the entire southern front
12/28/42	General Badanov's 24th Tank corps destroyed
1/1/43	25th Tank corps suffers same fate at Maryevka
1/25/43	Battle for Manychskaya; General von Schwerin's 16th I.D. (mot) stops Rotmistrov's push for Bataisk, thus keeping the bottleneck of Rostov open/Retreat of 1st Panzer army through Rostov
End of Dec. 1942 until end of January 1943	Disengaging from the Terek front, Groznyy-Mozdok to the Don
1/6/43	Battles of retreat on the Kuma, Soldato-Alexandrovskaya
January 43	1st Panzer army retreats to the Don
End of January 43	4th Panzer army retreats to Taganrog; 40th Panzer corps over the ice of the Sea of Asow
January 43	Withdrawal battles at Maykop-Krasnodar
1/4-2/2/43	Retreat of 17th Army from the Kaukasus and Kuban to the Gothic line Krasnodar-Taman peninsula
2/4/43	Russian attempt to land on the bay of Ozereyka fails; Successful landing in the bay of Zemess, Novorossisk, Myshkako mountain. Fighting for the "Little Country" lasts from February until November 1943
2/12/43	17th Army evacuates Krasnodar
February 43	Withdrawal to the Mius sector
2/15/43	Panzer corps Hausser evacuates Kharkov against Hitlers' orders
February 43	Defensive battle in the Mius sector
2/19-2/28/43	Manstein's backhanded counter attack destroys Red Armored Group Popov
3/15/43	Kharkov retaken by Panzer corps Hausser
3/18/43	Belgorod retaken by SS-Panzer corps
End of March 43	Russian offensive of Army group Vatutin fails; German front in the south still standing

VII. OPERATION "CITADEL"

7/4/43	4th Panzer army takes the heights of Jachontov-Streletskoye-Butovo-Gertsovka west of Byelgorod

7/5/43	9th Army (Model) starts attack from the north, south of Orel into the salient of Kursk; in the south the assault is being made by 4th Panzer army and Detachment Kempf from the previously gained heights. Heavy fighting for the Butyrki heights 253.5, Olchovatka heights 247, Teploye heights 272. Furious struggle for Cherkasskoye Korovino. Concentrated Russian air attacks on German airfields repelled by 8th Air corps (Seidemann)
7/8/43	Anti-tank group of 9th Battle Squadron destroys a Russian tank brigade and several infantry battalions from the air
7/11/43	4th Panzer army (Hoth) advances to Prokhorovka
7/12/43	Panzer battle of Prokhorovka
7/13/43	Fighting for the Donets crossings at Rzhavets-Alexandrovka. 9th army (Model) unable to take part in planned breakout to the south (North of Kursk). Situation: Russians gained deep penetrations in rear of 9th army
7/17/43	Operation "Citadel" abandoned. Withdrawal to starting point. Russians in hot pursuit

VIII. SCORCHED EARTH

8/5/43	Orel and Byelgorod retaken by the Russians
8/21/43	5th Russian Guard Tank army attack on Kharkov beaten back
8/22/43	Manstein orders evacuation of Kharkov
9/6/43	Soviets breaking through "Turtle position" on the southern front. Battle for Stalino and Mariupol
9/15/43	Retreat behind Dnieper and Desna. Scorched earth
9/22/43	Russian bridgehead on the Dnieper at Grigorovka and Bukrin
9/24/43	Destruction of Russian paratroopers in the area Grigorovka-Dudari-Bukrin by 24th Panzer corps (Nehring)
14-15 of Oct.43	Power station and dams of Zaporozhye blown
11/3/43	Army General Vatutin regrouping his Army group. German intelligence unaware. His surprise attack from the bridgehead of Lyutezh advances to Kiev
11/6/43	Kiev stormed by the Russians
11/7-11/12/43	General Rybalko grabs Fastov and Shitomir in the rear of Army group South
November 43	Counter attack of 48th Panzer corps stops Russian offensive in the vicinity of Fastov and Zhitomir
9/27-10/23/43	Fighting for the "Wodan" position (Melitopol)
10/23/43	Tolbuckin takes Melitopol
End of Oct/43	Fighting withdrawal of 6th Army to the Dnieper until Nov. Accesses by land to the Crimea are lost

IX. THE FRONT COLLAPSES

1/28-2/17/44	Encirclement of Cherkassy. Violent fighting for Swenigorodka-Korsun-Komarovka-Novaya Buda-Heights 239 Escape from Schanderovka to Lissyanka, crossing the Gniloy Tikich
3/16-4/6/44	Hube-cauldron of Uman-Vinnitsa-Kamenets-Poldolskiy. 1st Panzer army and parts of 4th Panzer army encircled
3/25/44	Manstein to see Hitler. Evacuation orders approved
3/29/44	Breakout battle begins. Crossing the Strypa, Hube fights his way through the Russians to the west
3/29/44	Cherniyenkov in the rear of 1st and 4th Panzer armies taken by Marshal Zhukov
3/30/44	Manstein replaced by Model
4/20-5/12/44	The Battle of the Crimea

5/9/44	Sevastopol lost
5/13/44	Final battle of the Crimean army
6/27/44	Begin of Russian major offensive against Army group Center
6/27/44	"Fortified Places" Vitebsk-Orscha-Mogilev and Bobruysk surrounded. Russians take Orscha
6/27/44	Vitebsk capitulates
7/3/44	Soviets take Minsk
7/4/44	One third of the Bobruysk garrison fights its way back
7/8/44	Baranovivhi in Russian hands
End of July 44	German front broken. Single corps and divisions break through to the west, "Wandering cauldrons." Russians reach the Vistula and the borders of East Prussia

The battle for the Reich begins

THE WAR IN RUSSIA
Photographed by the soldiers

Direction of captions for the photos refer to *Operation Barbarossa* or *Scorched Earth* (with chapter and page), both books written by Paul Carell: *Operation Barbarossa, The March to Russia,* and *Scorched Earth, Battles Between the Volga and Vistula.*

N

BARENTS—SEE

NORWEGEN

SCHWEDEN

Narvik

Kirkenes
Petsamo
Murmansk
Alakurtti
Salla
Kandalakscha
Kiestinki
Louchi

Rovaniemi

WEISSES MEER

Archangelsk

BOTTNISCHER BUSEN

FINNLAND
22. 23.6.1941 *

Petrosawodsk
Onega-
See

Ladoga-
See

Swir

OSTSEE

HELSINKI

STOCKHOLM

FINNISCHER BUSEN

Leningrad
Schlüsselburg
Tschudowo
Tichwin
Wolchow

Reval
Narwa
Nowgorod

Peipus
See
Pleskau

Ilmen-See
Star.-Russa
Cholm
Demjansk
Seliger-See
Welikije
Luki

Kalinin

Dwina

A—A LINIE

Rybinsker
Stausee

Wolga

Wetluga

Gorki

Riga

Libau

Welikaja
Lowat

Dünaburg

Düna

Witebsk

Rschew

MOSKAU

Wjasma
Kaluga

Oka

Tula

Kuibyschew

Königsberg

Danzig

ES
REICH

Memel

Kowno

Njemen

Smolensk

Berësina

Orscha

Minsk

Mogilew

Brjansk

Orel

SOWJET-UNION

Oka

Woronesch

Don

Medwjediza

Saratow

Bialystok

Bobruisk

Rogatschew

Weichsel
Bug

WARSCHAU

Brest-
Litowsk

General-
Gouvernement

Baranow

Oder

Pripjet-Sümpfe

Pripjet

Gomel

Desna

Sejm

Kursk

Bjelgorod

Charkow

Rossosch

Oskol

Kalatsch

Stalingrad

Tschir

Tschirskaja

Wolga

Wassiljewka

Myschkowa

Schitomir

Lemberg

Winniza

SLOWAKEI

WIEN

11.4.1941. *

Donau
BUDAPEST

UNGARN

Theiss

22.6.1941. *
RUMÄNIEN

BUKAREST

JUGOSLAWIEN

BELGRAD

Donau

Kanew

Kiew

Tscherkassy

Poltawa

Krementschug

Dnjepr

Dnjepropetrowsk

Stalino

Kam.Podolsk

Bug

Uman

Kriwoi Rog

Nikopol

Saporoschje

Taganrog

Rostow

Bataisk

Donez

Woroschilowgrad

Mius

Don Aksai

Astrachan

Kotelnikowo

Sal

Manytsch

Elista

KAS

Tschernowitz

Dnjestr

Nikolajew

Melitopol

Odessa

Pruth

Perekop

Asowsches
Meer

Kertsch

Krasnodar

Kuban

Kuma

Ischerskaja

Mosdok

Naltschik

Grosnij

Konstanza

BULGARIEN

SOFIA

19.4.1941. *

Eupatoria
KRIM
Simferopol
Sewastopol

Feodosia
Jalta

Noworossisk

Maikop

Tuapse

Elbrus

Terek

Tiflis

SCHWARZES MEER

Suchumi
Batumi

KEI

Legend:

Deutsches Reich 1941 mit Gene-
ralgouvernement, Verbündeten
und besetzten Gebieten

Neutrale Staaten

.... Ziel der Operation Barbarossa

* Tag des Kriegseintritts

I.
BLITZKRIEG AND BATTLES
OF ENCIRCLEMENT
Goal: Astrakhan-Archangelsk Line

They already crossed the Bug and advance to the Berezina. The vehicles carry the white G, tactical symbol of Panzergruppe Guderian. Everything looks like maneuver; Blitzkrieg and Blitzsieg. Dr. Türk's photo shows the war at the opening stage. It was like this, and was seen like it by countless soldiers. On June 22,1941 the advance unit of 3rd Panzerarmy south of Brest-Litovsk, and along the 1,600 Kilometer long front, Panzer and Infantry forded the rivers on the border, and broke through the fortifications of the Russian/German demarcation line. Hitler wanted to reach the Line Astrakhan-Archangelsk in eight weeks.

Berlin, 22. Juni. Das Oberkommando der Wehrmacht
gibt bekannt:

An der sowjetruffischen Grenze ist es seit den frühen
Morgenstunden des heutigen Tages zu Kampfhandlun-
gen gekommen.

Ein Versuch des Feindes, nach Ostpreußen einzudringen,
wurde unter schweren Verlusten abgewiesen. Deutsche
Jäger schossen zahlreiche rote Kampfflugzeuge ab.

**Roads and Bridges -
The Main Objective of Advance**
Soviet counter attack with light tanks on the
highway to Minsk is being stopped by anti-tank
units.

Generaloberst Guderian, creator and soul of the German Panzer forces during the battle for Smolensk. His motto: Panzer troops must be commanded from the front lines.

Feldmarschall Walter Model
Master of strategic defense. In the summer of 1941 the *Generalleutnant,* commander of 3th Panzer division, seen here at his advanced battle command post behind the Dnieper, south of Mogilev.

***Feldmarschall* Erich von Lewinski, von Manstein**
First Commander on the Northern Wing; Commanding General of 56th Panzer corps which took Dünaburg in a legendary raid. Then commanding 11th Army, which was used at every critical point during the war in Russia. Half of the Eastern Front was temporarily under his command. He became the most important strategist of the Second World War. Here with General Breith at the battle command post of 3rd Panzer corps during the battle of Kursk, south of Belgorod July 1943.

Assault Group Has Already Crossed the River
Leutnant Herbert Adam took this shot of the engineer bridge over the Dnieper at Orscha, while his 5th Panzer division prepared for a lunge in direction Vyazma. • Heavy infantry gun breaking down resistance of opposing positions.

Mud and Snow

Nobody knows mud, unless one experienced Russia in spring and fall. The dust, quagmire and snow are unforgettable for every soldier. ● (Top right) Cathedral of Smolensk after the first snow of 1941. ● 29 degree below Celsius — only a gasoline fire can start the motorcycle of a medic. Horse and sled in the background don't have this problem.

42/43

On the Highway to Moscow
Hauptmann Salchov titled his color photo "Mainstreet of Gschatsk in evening light" (Top left). ● The play of the settling winter sun tempted Alfred Trischler to take a shot of a small cloister in Vyasma (Bottom left).

Asmus Remmer took this photo December 1,
1941 in the village in front of Moscow; the
thermometer read 36 degrees below zero Celsius.

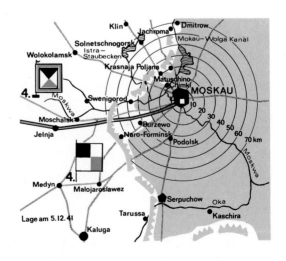

Lage am 5.12.41

Icy Eastern Front
On this frost-bitten Sunday morning,
soldiers of the 208th I.D. walk to the
mass in Schisdra. ● Self-propelled
assault gun giving cover. ● Assault
troop of Pomeranian 122nd I.D. held
down by enemy fire along the Memel.
An hour later, supplies roll over the
unscathed bridge.

Motorized Troops Set the Pace

Column after column of Panzer roll to the east: concentrated power, is the keyword. 3580 Panzers are ready to go. • At Taganrog General Kirchner's 1st Panzer division crosses the Yura, tributary of the Memel. The goal of Army Group North is Leningrad.

(*Operation Barbarossa*, page 196-209).

50/51

Ein Zugmelder

Fhj.Gefr. Dieter Prill
† 1941

Schütze Lothar Mallach

›Der Blaue‹   Gefr. Hans Müller

Ogfr. Robert Schm
† 1941

52/53

Jffz. Pawendenat
† 1941

Infantry Marches
In the searing sun behind the Panzerblitz; over dusty secondary roads into the endless
country. Lothar Mallach of Düsseldorf inscribes his photo: I'm the seventh man. 1st
company, 410th Infantry Regiment south of Kovno.

The First Prisoners

Crumbling under the impact of artillery fire, the Russian border troops give up. Their bewildered looks are caught by the camera. Parts of the Brest-Litowsk garrison were surprised from their sleep. • The Red soldiers raced in their underwear to the battle stations. Too late! One and a quarter hours after the war began, they walk into captivity. • Even a driver of a supply column ends his journey shortly after sunrise in a German advance unit. • (Lower right) The commander of an Air Force division, overrun by Germans, quarrels with his fate.
(*Operation Barbarossa*, page 11-14).

54/55

Face of the Encirclement Battles

Long columns of prisoners move to the west. ●
Commander-in-Chief of the 6th Soviet Army
General Lieutenant Musytschenko captured
(Upper right) ● The first signs of fanatic
resistance are showing; the inscription on the
wall of a casemate of the fortress Brest-Litovsk
reads: "I die, but I will not surrender. Good bye
homeland. 7/20/1941." ● Stalin's son, Lieutenant
Josef Stalin taken prisoner July 19, declared at
the first interrogation: "The leadership of my
division was stupid." He was a considerate and
self-confidant officer. Nothing is known about
his fate (Lower right).

The Many Faces of Blitzkrieg
German Nebelwerfer firing at a bunker life. The
15-cm. shells weighed 35 Kilo (70 lbs), the
fragmentation radius about 100 meters. • Low
flying Ratas chase motorcycle dispatcher of 4th
Panzer division on the road Bobruysk-Stary
Bychov. • Machine gun crew changing positions.

58/59

Victors Always Celebrate
July 1, 1941, Riga falls into German hands. Fast units of the 1st East Prussian corps stormed the city and kept the retreating Soviet armies away from Kurland. Fierce fighting for the bridges.
• Riga burns.

60/61

I had a comrade . . .
After crossing the Düna members of 19th Panzer
division, Lower Saxony, bury their dead in a mass
grave. ● Wounded are transported to the dressing
station

62/63

With Field-glass and Map
Marshal Zhukov still a General in 194[...]
still Stalin's top man, improvises t[...]
defense of Moscow (Upper left).
General Höpner, commander 4th Pan[...]
group views the coveted and seiza[...]
Leningrad from the heights of Duder[...]
(Lower left).

64/65

At the outset of war, every soldier met three well-known Soviet weapons: (Top to bottom) the Sewing Machine or I.V.D. (Ivan on duty) a primitive Soviet all-purpose plane. ● The single-seater Rata with two machine guns. ● The powerful KW-2 a 52-ton tank with 15.2-cm. cannon.

Dangerous Weeks
First effective opposition by
the Russians emerged during
the fighting for the Dnieper.
Especially dangerous were the
Soviet snipers in the trees,
picking out the officers of the
attacking German units. ●
(Right) Vicious combat in the
villages east of the Dnieper
marked Soviet resistance.
(From top to bottom) Scouting
vehicle. Personnel carrier.
Panzer III with 3.7-cm gun.

Infantry Attack

Crossing the Dnieper at Mogilev an enemy anti-tank gun fired at the same moment as Gerhard Tietz took his photo. The gun, standing behind a bush at the light sand spot, was taken minutes later by infantry. (Right) ● At the same time, Grenadiere of 19th Panzer division bridging the Düna cleared their way to Velikiye Luki. (Bottom left to right) Machine gun crew 37th Panzer-grenadierregiment at Dzisna. ● 47th Panzer-grenadierregiment fighting for Nevel. ● Mortar crew taking up position.

68/69

Bobruisk

Orel

Cities on the Wayside of War
How many German soldiers walked their streets?
Passed over their bridges? Into action, out of battle.
Advancing and then retreating. Bobruysk, city on
the Berezina. Orel, Capital of the Oka region. Rural
Bolchov, junction between Orel and Belev. The
beautiful Smolensk on both sides of the Upper
Dnieper with its old city walls from the 16th
century.

Smolensk

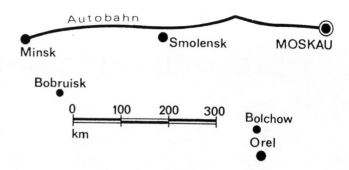

Autobahn

Minsk • ———————————— • Smolensk ◉ MOSKAU

Bobruisk •

0   100   200   300

km

Bolchow •

Orel •

Bolchow

A Quick Glance to the Window
Fieldpack on his back, shelter half and mess kit.
Gas mask clattering against the rifle. The rain
and the mud are here.

The cathedral of Vyasma was a place of pilgrimage for officer and soldier alike. ● *Feld-marschall* von Kluge, appointed commander of Army Group Center December 19, 1941, led the defensive battles of Moscow.

Warriors and the Warred Upon
A Ukrainian village sees German soldiers for the first time at the end of August 1941. ● A group of Moscovite tank hunters; a special detachment of the Red Army equipped with mine dogs. The dogs carried explosives on their backs, triggered on contact by crawling underneath the Panzer.
(*Operation Barbarossa*, pages 118-120).

Here We Go Again

Our artillery barrage rolls over us in direction of the enemy. ● Let's go! Gunners 2 and 3 are the ammunition carriers and gunner 1 with the machine gun while a Panzer IV gives cover. ● (Bottom left) Attention - enemy artillery positions. ● (Lower right) Digging in under fire; your life depends on your foxhole.

Marching to Romny
Panzer divisions supposed to take Moscow were ordered to the south, to participate in the Kiev encirclement. Armored personnel carrier with 3.7-cm. anti-tank gun (Upper right) and a self-propelled tank destroyer with 4.7-cm. cannon on the battlefield before Romny. ● (Left page) The village is taken. Careful! What's in the barn? ● Village classroom provides quarters (Bottom right).

Over Ukrainian Dust Roads

Endless the land. Rutted, crumbling roads. Columns engulfed by dust. ● Canteens are indispensable. ● Mobile filtration installations produce healthy drinking water from pools and creeks. ● The village well seemed to become an oasis.

Bravery of Men
A bunker and a steel cupola have to be smashed. (Left to right) Assault with flamethrower. ● After throwing a concentric charge inside, pressing on past the smoking ruins.

The First Cigarette
After fighting near Leningrad (Left). ●
(Bottom left) Russian prisoner at Uman.
● Advance unit resting somewhere in
Latvia (Right) ● The "Top" with
special rations for the men in action:
Cigarettes, cigars and candy.

84/85

Gschatsk

Wjasma

WITEBSK

Richtung Minsk

Gschatsk

Dmit

MOS

SMOLENSK

Wjasma

Borowsk

Malojarosslawez

MOGILEW

0   100   200   250
km

KALUGA

86/87

Mogilew

Borowsk

Dmitrow

Rollbahn nach Moskau

Malojaroslawez

On the Road to Moscow

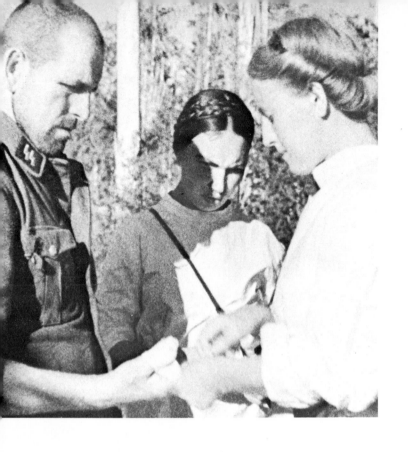

Women on the Other Side
A Russian female medic and nurse dressing a German prisoner • (Below left) Captured female member of a tank crew. • Shot through chest and back, a Soviet WAC is treated by a Soviet medic. • (Right page) *Hauptmann* Engelin, 3rd Infantry Regiment talks to captured female officers. • Russian staff aides in captivity.

88/89

The Marshal who Resembled Stalin
S.M. Budennyy, Commander-in Chief
without luck. Beaten at Uman; his
Army Group was destroyed in the battle
for Kiev. Budennyy and General Batow
(our photo above) at the command post
of the 65th Army. ● (Upper left) Narrow
escape from German encirclement. ●
(Lower left) Russian assault troops
attacking.

Orgy of Mud
Boots tied shut. • Troublesome haul for the ammunition carrier. • Motorcycle dispatcher on his way to the telephone station of the 197th I.D. • Infantry with a baggage cart on a secondary road towards the highway to Moscow.

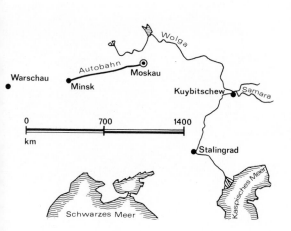

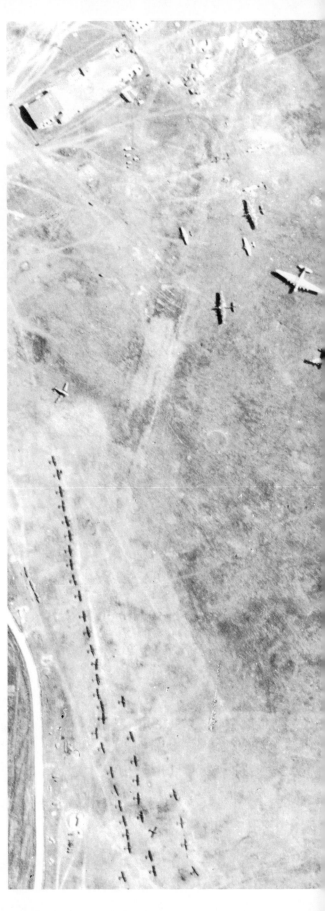

Moscow Under Siege
November 6, 1941, Stalin giving his
famous pep-talk in Moscow's Maya-
kovski Metro station. • (Lower left)
Military parade on the Red Square
November 7, 1941. • German long
distance reconnaissance planes photographed the airport of Kuybitschev —
temporary premises of the Soviet
government showing Stalin's plane
with fighter escorts, ready to take off.

TRABRENNBAHN

KREML

1:40000

bia Lfl.2

Scheinanlage
KREML ?

Only 100 Kilometer to Moscow
The middle of October, the 10th Panzer division passes the historic statue of Honor in Borodino, 110 Kilometer west of Moscow. ● Guide post of the 5th Panzer division: Moscow - 100 Kilometer! ● *Hauptmann* Salchov took this shot from the woods of Moschaisk on the old Postal road, 95 Kilometer to Moscow. ● This aerial picture of the Soviet Capital shows an interesting fact: 4.3 Kilometers north of the Kremlin the race-track area shows countless bomb craters. Why? Using fake houses and painted roofs for camouflage, the German bombers were being duped, and missed the Kremlin entirely.

96/97

Deep snow drifts had to be cleared
during a blizzard making life miserable.

II.
At Moscow's Gates

Siberian Cold and Siberian Regiments

Fourteen days previously, mild winter weather and light frost alloted the German offensive to start and thus forcing the fall of Moscow. Almost reaching the goal, General "Winter" appeared on the scene. Siberian cold smothered the land. This was not included in the Blitzkrieg schedule of the Germans. No winter clothing for the troops, no anti-freeze for weapons or vehicles. Stalin hurriedly brought in Siberian Regiments used to the cold from the Far East; believing his master spy Sorge, the Japanese would not attack Russia.

Trying from the South
Guderian's 2nd Panzer Army was supposed to force access to Moscow from the south. Driving through early morning fog, Panzers of the 29th corps ford the Upa, passing Tula to the north, on the 19th of November. Gerhard Tiets took this photo. Will the raid to the Moskwa be Successful?
(*Operation Barbarossa*, pages 136-149).

Panzer Assaulting Tula
Poorly camouflaged with watery whitewash, Guderian's Panzers try to break the stronghold around Tula. ● It snows every day and the landscape turns even more wintery.

Running Out of Fuel

Inside the Panzer it's bitter cold. The crews are taking more and more breaks to warm up. (Upper left) ● Tula is passed and Bolochovka with its important iron ore mines is reached. ● But then, no more gasoline and Soviet resistance grows stronger daily. Assemble. Wait.

102/103

Warming Fires
Life under a foreign sky at 30 below zero will
be reduced to the elementary basics. Fire now
plays the same main part as it did in the times
of primitive man. Without fire the soldier was
lost in the blood chilling iciness. (From left to
right) Guards at a factory wall in Istra. A fire
in an open field woke the spirits. ● Artil-
lerymen warming their hands on a permanent
fire besides their 10.5-cm. howitzer. ● Combatants of the III. detachment, 19th Artillery
Regiment (mot.) in the bitter fight for the area
south of Naro Fominsk. *Oberleutnant* Porzig
in the middle.

104/105

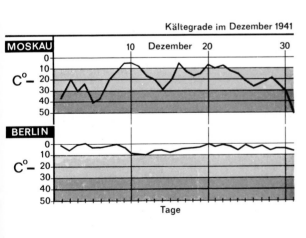

Kältegrade im Dezember 1941

MOSKAU

Dezember

C°–

BERLIN

C°–

Tage

41 Degrees Below Zero
Still no winter clothing. Anything
in the soldier's possession is worn;
on top of that went his great coat. No
fur cap, but a thin head protector,
under the forage cap or the ice-cold
steel helmet. The hob-nailed boots
are the worst; feet freeze very fast in
them. Self-made straw shoes are poor
compensation.

Snow, Yards High

The winter in front of Moscow was absolute hell for the horses. Only teams of them were able to supply the troops. The animals were used until they dropped of exhaustion. The total lack of precaution by the Supreme Command of Armed Forces, sending the divisions of Army Group Center into the winter offensive, is clearly demonstrated in these photos.

Last Ditch Efforts to Help the Front
Woolen clothes, furs, skis - everything the soldiers in Russia did not have, was collected in the homeland. A touching sacrifice without any practical consequences. ● (Lower right) Clothing arriving at the 122nd I.D.

People to Arms
Moscow mobilized the civilians. Worker battalions were formed, here saying good bye to
their families. After being dressed and armed,
they went into action in the nearby battle lines.
(Upper left and right) ● Losses of these brave but
inexperienced units are severe (Lower right). ●
Quickly raised tank obstacles were supposed to
stop German Panzers.
(*Operation Barbarossa*, pages 158-159).

The Enemy of the German Panzer

Day by day the Russian defense of Moscow grew more effective. The Red soldier still used the primitive Molotov cocktail - a gasoline-filled bottle with a fuse (Lower left). ● Successful anti-tank rifle battalions appeared (Lower right). ● Most dangerous of all: the Ratsch-Bumm, an all-purpose 7.62-cm. gun (Upper right). ● At Ilinskoye, a defensive position of Moscow, Soviet Ratsch-Bumm wiped out a full company of the 19th Panzer Division. (*Operation Barbarossa*, pages 130-132).

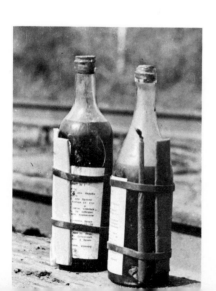

The Siberians are Coming

Clad in warm padded jackets, fur caps and felt boots the Siberian Regiments, experienced in winter fighting, storm and crawl toward the German attackers (Upper right, lower left). • Howling rocket salvos of the "Stalin-organs" smash the way for them. • Still in their summer uniforms German rear-guards with a light machine gun in the area of Burzevo.

Sabers Drawn
December 17, 1941, Dowator's Cossack Corps attacked over the River Rusa trying to shatter the front of 19th Corps on the highway to Moscow. ● Josef Bange, member of a machine gun crew, 20th Panzer Division, took this photo showing the defense against this attack. Bullets flail the snow of the frozen Rusa. ● And the dead bodies cover the ice. ● South of the highway German battle groups are also involved in heavy defensive fighting to prevent a break through of the Soviets.
(*Operation Barbarossa*, pages 288-292).

Village Changes into Battlefield

Evacuation, banishment, fugitive — three definitions of apocalypse in the 20th century. The poorest shack is still a home, and being driven out of it is a cruel blow of fate. Lomny, in the area of Korovino, experienced this misfortune.

Counterblows on All Fronts
Counter attacks are rolling everywhere in front of Moscow: area of Kaluga (Top left). ● At Kalinin on the Upper Volga. ● On the Leningrad front. ● Guderian's Panzers are stopped at Tula by General I.W. Boldin's 50th Army. The German blitz is broken.
(*Operation Barbarossa*, pages 149-174).

Retreat

The Russian storms against the badly shaken German frontlines (Below). ● German rearguards slow down the advance and cover the withdrawal. ● But what a retreat: burning houses, smashed vehicles on both sides of the road on which the divisions endure their way to the west, as seen in this picture. Neighborhood of Tula-Orel (Top left and center). ● Highways turned into ice-rinks. Instead of spreading sand, hay, which the wind blew away, was used.

Daily Bread of the Soldiers

The German Army now made a distinction in the rationing of food. Basic food was the same for everyone — soldier or general. It was different in the Soviet Army. Klaus Pein's picture had the title: "Still-life of blood sausages." ● Every Division had a butcher company. ● The field-kitchen or "Goulash-Cannon" was equipped with a heated cooking kettle, water reservoir, frying pan and heating pane. Very simple but exceedingly able to work close to the front.

Tagesverpflegung des Soldaten: Hauptnahrungsmittel

Brot	650 g	Marmelade	200 g
Butter oder Fett	45 g	Bohnen Kaffee	5 g
Wurst oder Käse	120 g	Kaffee-Ersatz	10 g
Frischfleisch	120 g	Zigaretten	6 Stück

What's Going on in the Village?
Only a picture — but Hitler is present. His predecessor Stalin had a shrine decorated with flowers. ● Arrival of a German combine for the farmers in notorious Katyn is more realistic. ● Land is being distributed in the Kursk-Orel region — but the rifle is still visible.

This photo shows the Lower Don with its wide, wooded river valley near Konstantinovka. In the foreground Rasdorskaya. The summer of 1942 saw many German divisions fording the river, driving towards the Caucasus.

FALL BLAU

Führerweisung Nr:41

Spätere Ziele

134/135

Don't forget to salute behind front lines!
Caught by Asmus Remmer: It's thawing. A
village behind the front. Mired roads, saluting
Landser, recruited women. ● The vignette of
Alfred Ott from Ordanivka shows the contrast of
summer.

Dr. Ott snapped this photo during the days when
the 6th Army forded the Don at Kalatsch and
moved in the direction of Stalingrad: the Don
near the delta of the Sea of Asov. Peaceful mood.

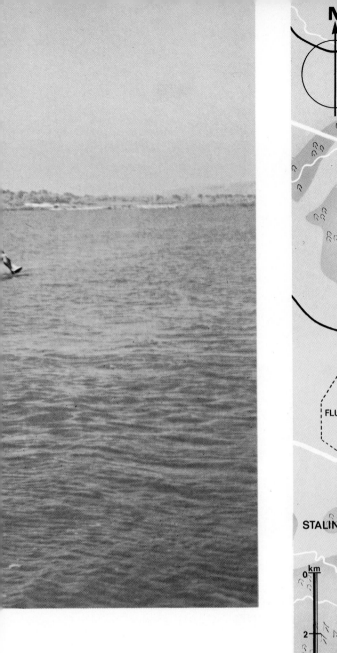

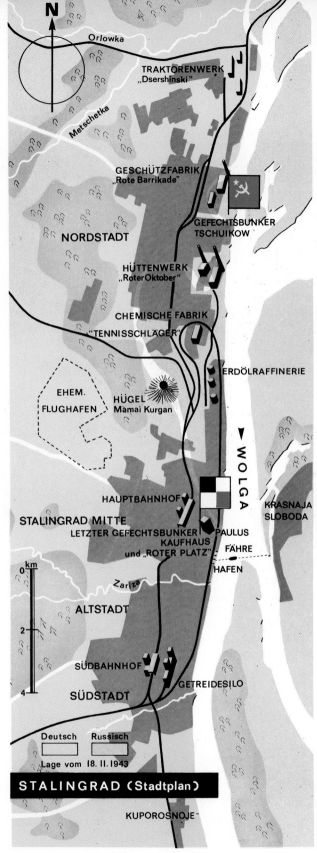

N

Orlowka

TRAKTORENWERK
„Dsershinski"

Metschetka

GESCHÜTZFABRIK
„Rote Barrikade"

GEFECHTSBUNKER
TSCHUIKOW

NORDSTADT

HÜTTENWERK
„Roter Oktober"

CHEMISCHE FABRIK
"TENNISSCHLÄGER"

ERDÖLRAFFINERIE

EHEM.
FLUGHAFEN

HÜGEL
Mamai Kurgan

W
O
L
G
A

KRASNAJA
SLOBODA

HAUPTBAHNHOF

STALINGRAD MITTE
LETZTER GEFECHTSBUNKER
KAUFHAUS
und „ROTER PLATZ"

PAULUS

FÄHRE

HAFEN

Zariza

ALTSTADT

0 km

2

SÜDBAHNHOF

GETREIDESILO

4

SÜDSTADT

Deutsch	Russisch

Lage vom 18. II. 1943

STALINGRAD (Stadtplan)

KUPOROSNOJE

138/139

When Alfred Ott took this picture, he saw the men
crying from the cold: Italian soldiers from the warm
south of Europe, in the merciless hell of a blizzard.
● This phot of the industrial surroundings of Krivoy
Rog, taken by Günther Thiem, shows clearly that the
burden of rebuilding rested on the shoulders of the
Russian woman.

The 2nd Battery, Anti-aircraft Regiment 5 of Munich with
their 88mm guns near Murmansk, at the Fischer peninsula.
This photo was shot in the summer of 1941. Murmansk,
backdoor to the Atlantic, was one object in the very first
preparations for the war against Russia. Its harbor and
railways received the American shipments which reinforced
the Soviet resistance decisively. To prevent this, German
Gebirgsjäger and the Finnish Corps fought their own special
war. The Divisions of Army Group North operated south of
Lake Ladoga.

T 34 1943

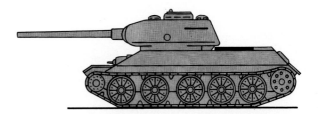

Characteristic scene of the
woods on the Volkhov. ●
German submarine in the
Baltic Sea off Danzig.

German Armies of Army Group South marching over the Pruth (Above), over Dneiper and Don.

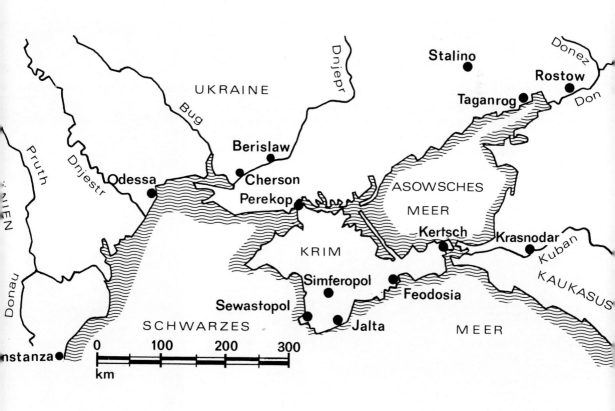

Unguri

M

III.
Storm on the Southern Wing
Crossing the great rivers in the direction of the Caucasus and Stalingrad

146/147

Broad rivers flow through the vastness of southern Russia. Hitler's Blitzkrieg swept over Dnestr, Bug, Dnieper on schedule. On to the Crimea! Over the Mius! Increasing Russian defense at the end of 1941, stopped the advance of the German Southern Wing. The Lower Don became the watershed of victory. Rostov broke the German tempest. Hitler shifted the decision to 1942: "Operation Blue" earmarked for triumph in the south. Our photo shows the Lower Don with its wide, wooded river valley near Konstantinovka. In the foreground Rasdorskaya. The summer of 1942 saw many German Divisions fording the river, driving towards the Caucasus.

E

New-Podolsk

Bronita

Into the Boats
Rivers are not insurmountable objects. Imbued with the precision of a fine clockwork, even if the bridges were blown. The troops had instructive photos with marked enemy positions (Above) (E = Attention - enemy bunkers with casemats). ● Divisions of the 11th Army cross the Dnestr. Well camouflaged infantry and engineers wait for their order: into the boats (Right). The inflatable rafts hold twelve men.

Over the Dnieper
Almost three and a half Kilometers wide, the second
largest river of Eastern Europe. German Grenadiers
crossing on July 10-11 were not aware of the decisive
role the river played in the outcome of the war.
(*Operation Barbarossa*, pages 67-80).

Retreating Red soldiers used the skeleton from a Cherson grammar school, as a warning salute to the advancing Germans. But the soldiers laughed and left him standing. • Forty-eight hours later the salute turned into reality. Advance unit Janus burying their dead. • An eighty-eight shell hit this Russian supply vehicle, and Walter Hackl titled his snapshot: ''Dead and bread loaded'' (Lower right).

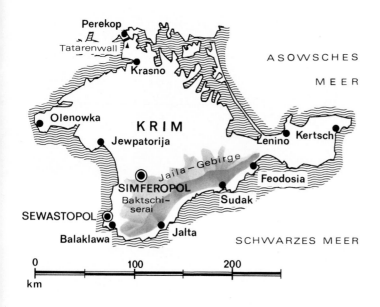

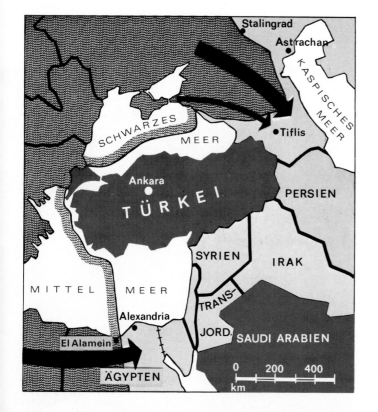

Fighting for Paradise

"Who owns the Crimea, controls the Black Sea and decides the politics of Turkey." Hitler's try to gain entry to the Crimea late summer 1941, followed the same motto. But it failed. German assault troops were tied down at the entrance to Paradise, at Perekop and in the tank traps of the Tartar wall. The map shows the importance played by Turkey in Hitler's strategy of the "Big oil pincers" to engulf the Caucasus and the Near East. (*Operation Barbarossa*, pages 241-252).

154/155

Motorcycle Detachments to the Front
Hussars of the motorized Divisions liked the Southern Wing for its ideal battlefields. Sidecars marked with the "Jumping Horse", tactical emblem of the 24th Division, the battalion races into the steppe. Meets the enemy. "Get down." Attacks with machine gun and small arms. This photo was taken during the summer battles of 1942 on the way to the Don.

Inside, Outside
No soldier has a permanent quarter during any given war. He only has a temporary stay. A witness: the ''Berliner Morgenpost'' in the quarters of a Berlin Division (Below)

156/157

Walter Hackl wrote on this picture of a Tartar woman: "These women were pretty and proud, spitting at the feet of any approaching Landser."
• Beautiful Alushta on the Crimea with Jayla mountains in the background, seen from the road to Simferopol (Lower right).

N

← Belbek

Wolga

Stalin

Ural

Sibirien

← Ölberg

GPU

Molotow

← Maxim Gorki   Tscheka

S E W E R N A J A   B U C H T

Nord-Fort

SÜD BUCHT

SEWASTOPOL

S C H W A R Z E S

Sewernaja
Kossa

M E E R

Chersones ↘

Sapun

Friedhof

Strongest Fortress of the World
Like Moscow and Leningrad, Sevastopol withstood the German onslaught
in fall and winter of 1941. (Left) The heights around the historic fortress were
loaded with fortifications. ● Marines held the harbour. ● German railroad
guns with giant 80-cm. shells shattered the strongest casemats.
(*Operation Barbarossa*, pages 248-268).

158/159

Sevastopol Taken
Early summer 1942, Manstein's 11th Army
took the fortress by storm. For five days the fire
of 1,300 guns devastated fortifications and
outposts. Army Artillery destroyed the under-
ground steel cupolas of the 30.5-cm. batteries
(Top right). ● The important heights of
Sapun were taken by Grenadiers of the 170th
I.D., with the support of Nebelwerfer.
(*Operation Barbarossa*, pages 408-419).

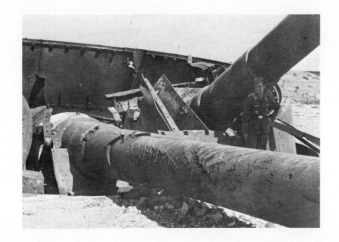

Above and Below the Ground

While Red troops fought in the battered positions, weapons and ammunition production kept going in subterranean galleys to the very last moment (Above). ● Center of command, and council of war, nerve centers of the costal Army, were located in underground casemates of the harbor (Left to right):J. Khuchnov, J. Petrov, and M. Kuznetsov. ● Sevastopol fell into German hands on July lst. Pockets of resistance continued until July 9th (Right) Romanian Artillery rolls into the city.

Drama at Feodosia
November 3, 1941 marked the fall of
Feodosia, eastern part of the Crimea.
(Above) ● But a landing of powerful
Soviet Armed Forces surprised the
Germans at Kertch and the rear of
the peninsula at Feodosia (Right). ●
Graf Sponeck, (photo from 1941, with
Major Zürn) Commanding General
of the 42nd Corps took the weak 46th
I.D. and evacuated the peninsula of
Kertsch. For this he was sentenced to
death, then pardoned, and ultimately
in 1944 he was executed by firing
squad. The 105th Infantry Regiment
of the 72nd I.D. stormed Feodosia
again on January 18, 1942.
(*Operation Barbarossa*, pages
252-268).

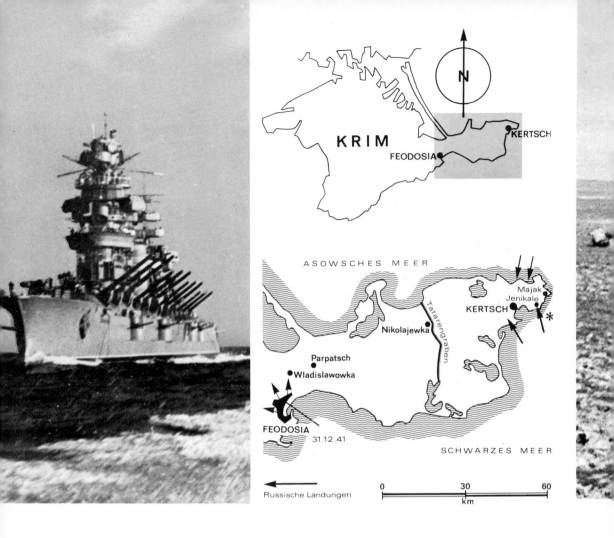

KRIM

KERTSCH

FEODOSIA

ASOWSCHES MEER

Majak
Jenikale
KERTSCH

Tatarengraben

Nikolajewka

Parpatsch

Wladislawowka

FEODOSIA
31.12.41

SCHWARZES MEER

Russische Landungen

0   30   60
         km

*

Jenikale

Opassnaja

Russische Landung

The Bloody Coast
The peninsula of Kertch held a key-point of German strategy: 1941/1942-springboard to the Caucasus; 1943-backbone of the Kuban bridgehead. (left) Battleship "Sevastopol." Supported by naval forces, Soviet landing troops tried again and again to gain a foothold.

"What you obliterate now, is no obstacle later on."
Hitler explains to General von Salmuth. Visit by the Führer at the Headquarters of Army Group South near Poltawa, June 1, 1942. The military heads of the Southern Wing meet in front of the situation map. Favorable development south of Kharkov compels Hitler to change the timetable of "Operation Blue." (*Operation Barbarossa*, pages 400-408). • (Left to right) General Schmundt, *Generaloberst* von Weichs; Hitler talking to General von Salmuth; in front of the map: General von Sodenstern, General von Mackensen, *Generaloberst* von Kleist; (half way covered) *Feldmarschall* Keitel conversing with General Paulus; *Generaloberst* of the Air Force Löhr.

Storming Rostov
Rostov was blitzed by units of Panzer Group Kleist on November 21, 1941. It took the Russians only one week to take the doorway to the Caucasus back (Left), and throw the Germans out. Eight months later, July 25, 1942 the Germans are back again. *Oberst* Reinhardt with 421st Infantry Regiment during the street-fighting.
(*Operation Barbarossa*, pages 268-272).

170/171

The White "K"
Taking revenge on July 25, 1942, for November 28, 1941, the 1st Panzer Army, the old Panzer Group Kleist, snatched the city again. Soviet Artillery tried without success to smash the jump-off positions of the German Panzers. ● Combat engineers mounted on Panzers advance to the city center (Right). ● Pockets of resistance in the ruins are mopped up by Panzer-grenadiers (Above).

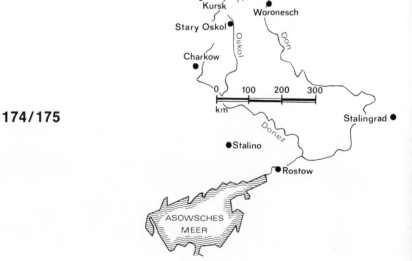

To the south . . .
Passage to the Caucasus is forced wide open.
Crossings over the Lower Don are gained.
Divisions of Army Group A and B storm to the
south,and east to the Volga.

174/175

Over the Chir, Over the Kshen

Are the Russians surrounded? The march on Stalingrad begins. First goal: Voronezh. Gun crew member 1 shoulders his machine gun again. • Platoon leader points out the direction. • Grenadiere, engineers and motorcycle riflemen attack. • In the center of it General Kempf, 48th Panzer Corps, in his command vehicle bearing the insignia of the Corps.

Rollbahn (Highway) 17 to Voronezh
July 28, 1942. Hoth's 4th Panzer Army
encounters Soviet opposition in front of
Voronezh. The Russian Artillery lays down a
curtain of fire. "Take cover"! Horses shy. The
battle rolls. ● Highway 17 is bordered by
graves.
(*Operation Barbarossa*, pages 420-434).

The Fateful City
Voronezh seen through the periscope (Left); an interesting photo taken by Walter Seelbach in an observation post of Heavy Artillery Detachment 635. ● City on the Don traffic junction and armament center became the pivot point of the summer offensive. After heavy losses, Grenadiers of the 16th I.D. (mot.), and the 3rd (mot.) were able to take the western part of the city.
(*Operation Barbarossa*, pages 430-433).

Trench Warfare in Voronezh

Every meter of ground in Voronezh had to be fought for. Out of shell craters trenches and earthen bunkers, like the great materiel battles of the first world war. Watching the opponent through a trench periscope beside the machine gun position. ● Lifting the head too high is dangerous; there are Soviet snipers like V. Kozlov, just being decorated by his Political commissar for his 30th kill.

Keep Going!
Again and again, somebody drops. But you
have to keep moving, push on. Orel stays
behind. Kursk and Kharkov, too. Voronezh.
Rostrov. Over the Don: to the east and south,
through steppes and fields of corn.

IV.
Stalingrad
"Every Soldier a Fortress"

The drama of Stalingrad has dawned. Nobody anticipated it, because the city was hardly considered in the plans of the German Supreme Command. Center of armament, and a harbor on the Volga, elimination and being brought under a "Force of Arms" was the foreseen fate of the city. The simple security action turned into a crippling defeat, and was the result of underestimating the adversary. Soldiers of the 62nd Soviet Army swore to General Zhukov, Stalingrad defender: "Every soldier a fortress" — and they kept their oath.

X-time: 5 O'clock
3 minutes to go. Light anti-tank gun ready to give coverage. The company leader already on top of the ditch. ●
Now it's time! ● Someone in the 3rd platoon keels over: "Medics"! ● They are there, helping. If the man had been one step closer, there would have been nothing left to help.

Kharkov
More than twenty German Divisions took part in the four battles for Kharkov. At least one million of them set foot into the fourth largest city of the Soviet Union. Pyramids of signposts guided them. ● They admired the monuments and buildings of Red Square. ● Trains and canals fulfilled important necessities in the economic structure of the country. Magnificent buildings stood beside hovels and beautiful churches.

Rossosch Falls
Anyone who marched with the troops of the 6th Army south of Woronesch, remembers Windmill Hill and the dusty highways on the passage to the Don. • Second part of "Operation Blue" started July 6th with a rapid advance into the bend of the Don to encircle the Russians (Right); Windmill Hill appears again in the background.
(*Operation Barbarossa*, pages 433-435).

192/193

Over the Chir to the Don
General Paulus outmaneuvered the Soviet forces in front of the Don. His Panzer Divisions gain passage over the Chir (Left). ● The Russians are badly hit by Stukas of 8th Air Force Corps. ● July 26, and German advance units are on the river within the wide Don bend.
(*Operation Barbarossa*, pages 479-482).

The Steppe of the Don
Two Panzer Corps spearhead the 6th Army. Infantry, horse-drawn artillery and equipment behind them. Objective: Kalatsch on the Don.
(*Operation Barbarossa*, pages 477-479).

194/195

The Bridges Over the Don

The technical machinery of the bridge-building combat engineers worked excellently. Colorful signposts of the Don heights were famous. ● Attacked 67 times in one night by Russian planes, the Luchensky bridge led into the bridge-head of the 11th Corps (Lower Right).

Donhöhenstrasse

Donbrücke Akatow

8 km Donbrücke Akimowskij

5 km Donbrücke Lutschenskij

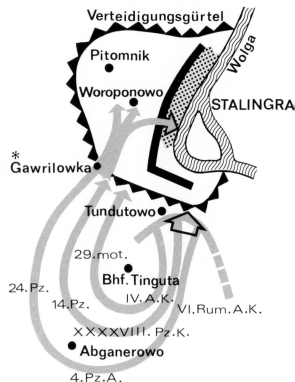

Breakthrough at Gavrilovka
Abganerovo on the outer defense ring of
Stalingrad was reached on August 19, 1942
by the 4th Panzer Army. (Below) ●
Grenadiers of the 29th I.D. storm positions
of the 64th Soviet Army (Right). ● Then it
stops. Hoth gambles on a bold regrouping,
and eleven days later, tears into the inner
defenses from the south-west. Still 13 Kilometers to Stalingrad.
(*Operation Barbarossa*, pages 486-493).

Verteidigungsgürtel
Pitomnik
Woroponowo
Wolga
STALINGRA
* Gawrilowka
Tundutowo
29.mot.
24.Pz.
Bhf. Tinguta
14.Pz.
IV.A.K.
VI.Rum.A.K.
XXXXVIII. Pz.K.
Abganerowo
4.Pz.A.

Durchbruch bei Gawrilowka am 30.8.1942 ✳

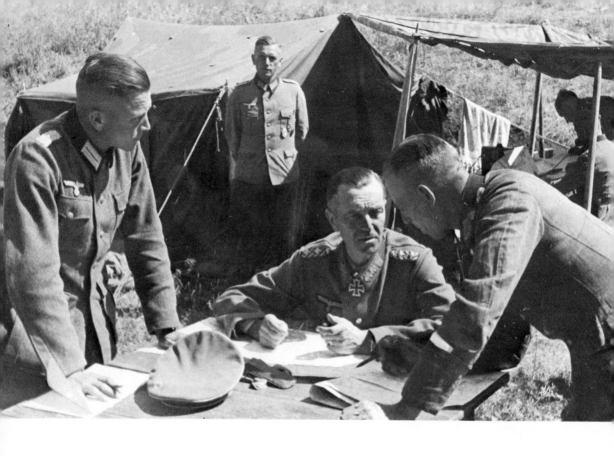

The Thrust Into the City

"A plan prepared in an Army tent thousands of miles away, decides victory" is an old Chinese proverb, often cited by Mao Tse-Tung. (Left) Battle Command post, 6th Army infront of Stalingrad. On the map table General Paulus, bent towards him General Rodenburg, Commander of the 76th I.D.; on the left *Oberstleutnant* Elchlepp the Ia. ● German armored forces break into the northern part of the city on September 9th ● On September 14, the 71th I.D. is already fighting in the center of town. ● The focal point of the fighting is the Grain Elevator, which is so very close for the taking. ● An arm shield, showing this elevator, was designed by General Paulus, to be worn by all soldiers of the 6th Army after the victory.

Combat in the City

The Photos on the three following pages are from the estate of *Generalfeldmarschall* Paulus, portraying the merciless fighting against constantly increasing resistance of the 62nd Soviet Army. ● Stalingrad, the fiery maelstrom in which the warriors were born. ● October arrives. A machine gun goes into position. The tripod for the heavy machine gun is carried by the rifleman on the right.

Into the Town of "Barrikady"
"We'll do it this way: First platoon
left, second right." ● Fast sprint over
open ground.

The Arms Plant
Saxons and Hessians of the 14th Panzer Division
and the 389th I.D. force their way through the
assembly halls of the arms manufacturing plant
"Red Barricade."
(*Operation Barbarossa*, pages 500-505).

The Dying City

Burned, smashed, windowless, enshrouded by gloomy clouds of smoke, that's the way a Soviet reporter sees Stalingrad on the steep western shore of the Volga. ● Trying to leave the city under artillery fire a few women with their last belongings hurry through the desolated streets. ● Ravines, ditches and caves are the last resorts for the civilian population.

Winter Arrives in Stalingrad

And the fighting still rages in the city. Soviet troops protect every meter of ground with fanatic obstinacy. "Giving up the city would destroy the moral of our people. Either we hold Stalingrad, or die here." Sworn by General Zhukov to Nikita Khrushchev and General Yeremenko September 12, 1941.

Historical Documents of the Last Act

On November 19, 1941, the 6th Army assembled to attack the last strongholds on the Volga. 4 Soviet Armies and 1 Tank Corps pierced the Romanian positions north-west and south of Stalingrad, and raced to close the pincers at Kalatch. The 6th Army is encircled. (*Operation Barbarossa*, pages 506-516).

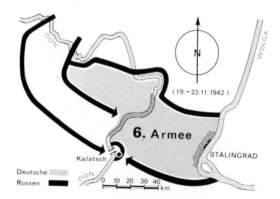

(19. – 23. 11. 1942)

6. Armee

Kalatsch

STALINGRAD

Deutsche
Russen

0 10 20 30 40
km

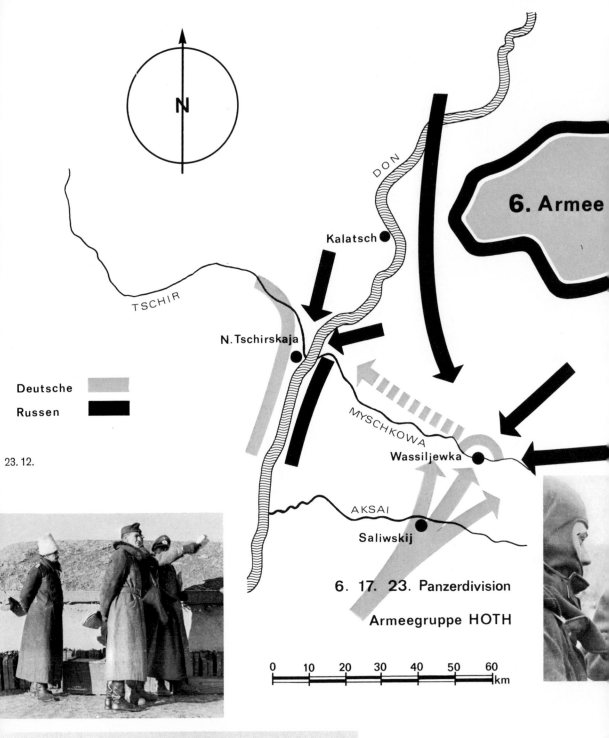

N

DON

Kalatsch

6. Armee

TSCHIR

N. Tschirskaja

Deutsche

Russen

23. 12.

MYSCHKOWA

Wassiljewka

AKSAI

Saliwskij

6. 17. 23. Panzerdivision

Armeegruppe HOTH

0   10   20   30   40   50   60
km

24. 12.

214/215

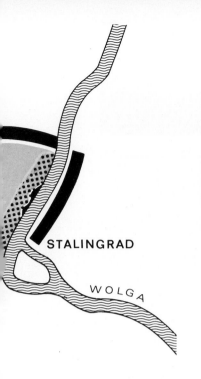

STALINGRAD

WOLGA

Relief Attack

Generaloberst Hoth is ordered to relieve 6th Army. Ahead of him are 100 Kilometers. On December 12 it starts: directives for the assault are given to the 11th Panzer Regiment ● December 14, the Regiment crossed the Aksaiy river. Long-barelled Panzer IV's stand on the other shore. ● Hoth's spearheads are 50 Kilometers from Stalingrad on December 22 and 23; Regimental Commanders and General Kirchner (with forage cap) and Raus discuss battle reports. The 8th Italian Army is overrun. ● To prevent a new catastrophe on the Chir, Hoth has to divert his strong armored forces. The Germans in Stalingrad can only wait in their snow caves.

12. 12.

22. 12.

14. 12

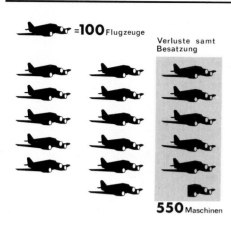

Verluste samt Besetzung

550 Maschinen

= **100** Flugzeuge

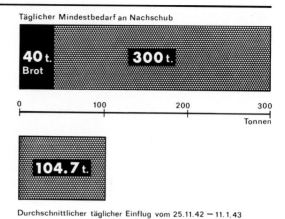

Täglicher Mindestbedarf an Nachschub

40 t. Brot	**300 t.**

0   100   200   300

Tonnen

104.7 t.

Durchschnittlicher täglicher Einflug vom 25.11.42 — 11.1.43

Winter - A Stronger Opponent

Supplying an Army under Siberian weather conditions proved to be impossible. Luftflotte 4 was beaten by this weather. Goods flown into the city never filled the mess kits enough to retain the fighting strength of the troops; not enough fuel to try a break-out. One third of the planes were lost. ● Time was on the Soviets side. Stubbornly defending the ruins, and regaining more and more strong points for their snipers; this old factory ruin for example.

Mysterious Caves
The Russians received their supplies and replacements over the frozen ice of the Volga. If the ice was broken the provisions came in boats and on floats. ● Out of reach of the German Artillery the steep western shore, ''secret weapon'' of the defenders, was the location for Staffs, hospitals, ammunition dumps and collecting points. (*Operation Barbarossa*, page 503).

Dynamos of Resistance
(Left) Nikita Khrushchev, General Chuyanov and General Yeremenko. (Below left to right) General Zhukov and General Gurkov.

The End
The wounded froze to death, the corpses grew stiff. ● Survivors surrendered. Straw boots made by the men were taken away to feed the Russian horses.

(From left) General Lattmann, 14th Pz. Div. ● General Sanne, 100th I.D. ● General Dr. Korfes, 295th I.D. ● General v. Seydlitz-Kurzbach, 2th A.K. ● General Magnus, 389th I.D. ● General Rodenburg, 76th I.D. ● General Leyser, 29th I.D. (mot) ● General Pfeffer, 4th A.K. ● General Vassol, Arko 153 ● General von Lenski, 24th Pz. Div. ● *Generaloberst* Strecker, 11th A.K. Page 216/217 continued: During the night of February 2, *Generaloberst* Strecker sits in the Command Post of the Battle Group Oberstleutnant Julius Müller. As morning dawns, Strecker says: "I'll have to go now." Müller understands: "l will do my duty." Fighting stops in the Northern cauldron at daylight. At 8:40 a.m. Strecker wires to *Führerhauptquartier*: "The six divisions of the 11th Army Corps fulfilled their duty." Out of ruins and ditches, hollow-eyed, starving men fall into grey columns, and are led into the steppe. Seemingly endless echelons. How many?
(*Operation Barbarossa*, page 548).

222/223

STALINGRAD: Verlustliste der 6. Armee

† = 6 000   Mann

18.12.1942

Verpflegungsstärke der im Kessel befindlichen deutschen und verbün = deten Truppen

230 300   Mann

Bis zum 24.1.1943

werden ausgeflogen (Verwundete und Spe = zialisten)   42 000

Bis zum 29.1.1943

gefangen   * 16 800

171 500   Mann

31.1.1943 – 3.2.1943

* 91 000 gehen in Gefangenschaft

80 500 Tote und Verwundete bleiben auf dem Schlachtfeld

Gefangene

107 800   Mann

Heimkehrer

6 000   Mann

* Sowjetische Angaben

General Rodimzev, head of the Stalingrad Guard announces the destruction of the 6th German Army in the "Red Square." What was left of the 6th Army lay as scrap in the streets of the dead city. ● Finnish Regiment "Turoma", famous for it fighting ability, marches along the mountain road in the vicinity of Kiestinki.

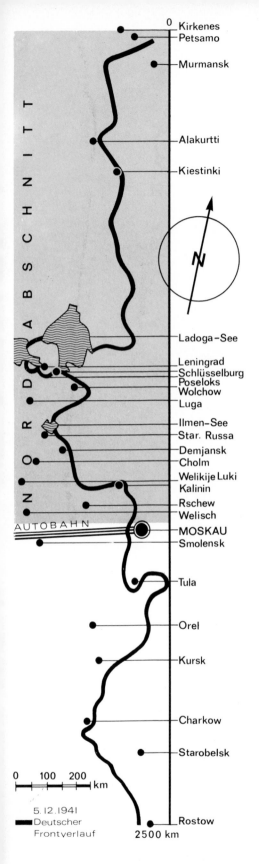

0 ─ Kirkenes
─ Petsamo
─ Murmansk

─ Alakurtti

─ Kiestinki

N

─ Ladoga-See

─ Leningrad
─ Schlüsselburg
─ Poseloks
─ Wolchow
─ Luga

─ Ilmen-See
─ Star. Russa
─ Demjansk
─ Cholm
─ Welikije Luki
  Kalinin
─ Rschew
─ Welisch
AUTOBAHN ─ MOSKAU
─ Smolensk

─ Tula

─ Orel

─ Kursk

─ Charkow

─ Starobelsk

0   100   200
├──┼──┼──┤ km

5.12.1941
▬ Deutscher
Frontverlauf

─ Rostow
2500 km

V.
Battles on the Northern Wing
Between the Arctic Ocean and Lake Seliger

War at the Edge of the World

Machine gun nest built from prehistoric rocks. The lifeless Tundra was the battleground of 139th Gebirgsjäger Regiment; stage for snipers and hand grenade duels. ● Combatants lived in caves erected from stones, mosses and sods. ● To supply the Arctic front Organization Todt had to build roads first.

(*Operation Barbarossa*, pages 364-385).

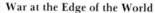

16,5 Mill.t. = 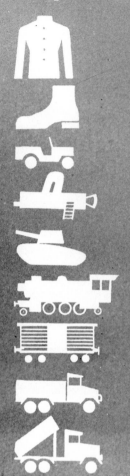 **2660**

Uniformtuche	90 Mill. Meter
Soldatenstiefel	11 Mill. Paar
Jeeps	50 000
Maschinengewehre	135 000
Panzerfahrzeuge	13 000
Lokomotiven	1 045
Güterwagen	7 164
LKW	427 284
Kipp u. Tankfahrzeuge	1 000

228/229

Versenkt 1,5 Mill. t. = 77

Deutschland ging in den Ostkrieg mit:	Flugzeuge	1 830
	Panzer	3 580
	motor. Fahrzeuge aller Art	600 000
Im 1. Kriegsjahr lieferten die Alliierten über Murmansk – Archangelsk:	Flugzeuge	3 052
	Panzer	4 048
	motor. Fahrzeuge aller Art	520 000
In der Schlacht um Kiew Herbst 1941 verloren die Russen:	Panzer	900
	Kraftfahrzeuge	15 000
	Geschütze	3 000

American relief shipments almost equalized Soviet losses of materiel.
From 1941 to 1945, American convoys delivered war materiel through the North Atlantic, to Murmansk and Archangelsk, value — 39 billion Deutschmarks. 14,700 planes, 7,000 tanks, 375,000 vehicles. On many Russian front line sectors, starting in 1942, 30% of Soviet transportation muscle was provided by American vehicles.

Guards at the Backdoor

Red Fleet submarines and minesweepers guarded Murmansk, protecting convoys from the West against German U-boats. (Right) Soviet sub leaving its base to collect a convoy bound for Murmansk. ● (Below) Commander Nikolas Lunin (three medals) and crew after their attack on the German battleship "Tirpitz" in spring 1942. ● (Left) Ships of the Lend-Lease fleet, which transported American war materiel. (*Operation Barbarossa*, pages 382-383).

Tägliche Brotration   1941/42

		Normalbrot
	1500 g	
LENINGRAD		
Arbeiter	250 g	
Angestellte Familienangehörige	125 g	
DEUTSCHLAND		
Erwachsene	325 g	
Jugendliche	375 g	
Kinder	245 g	

Every day 10,000 tons of supplies had to be flown into West-Berlin, during the "Airlift Crisis" of 1948/49, for the two and a half million inhabitants. Leningrads population of more than two million received no more than 86 tons daily. This was less then 1/10 of Berlin's rations.

Two and a Half Slices of Bread Daily.
Frozen Lake Ladoga was the only connection to the outside world from Leningrad (Above). The dangerous ice road was christened "Road of Life" by the Russians, passable only at night. Hunger brutalized the city. People collapsed in the streets and died (Left). ● Dead bodies were collected for burial in mass graves of the Volkhov cemetery.
(*Operation Barbarossa*, pages 222-240), and (*Scorched Earth*, pages 183-191).

Porogi Lays Across the River
At this point, the frozen Neva is 250 meters wide. Not
really a lot when the Russians stormed over the bank and
the ice shouting "Urrae." Private Hans Dornhofer took
this rare shot in spring of 1943 from the dug-out of an
observation post of the 100th Gebirgsjäger Regiment.
Corpses of fallen Russians are still there from the last
attack. ● The men of the 170th I.D. built their billets with
great skill, in the vicinity of Pulkovo. First entrance -
company office; second - quarters and the third, into the
kitchen.

The Outskirts of Leningrad
The Neva-front — Schlüsselburg-Gorodok-
Dubrovka —along, restless, highly hazardous
section. Ceaseless counter attacks to wipe out
penetrations of the Soviets (Top left). ● Very
lights demand artillery support. Volunteers of
the Spanish "Blue Division", suffered harsh
losses. Here they bury their dead in front of
Leningrad in the spring of 1943.
(*Operation Barbarossa*, pages 349, and
Scorched Earth, pages 191-222).

The Volkhov

Dead woods and smashed positions. ● Fortified islands in the
swamp could only be supplied by rubber boats. ● The gloomy
front in the primeval landscape of the Volkhov. It was one of
the bloodiest battlefields on the Easern Front, and both sides
sustained very heavy losses. Close combat and hand grenades
kept the enemy in check both day and night.

(*Operation Barbarossa*, pages 361-363 and *Scorched Earth*,
pages 205-222).

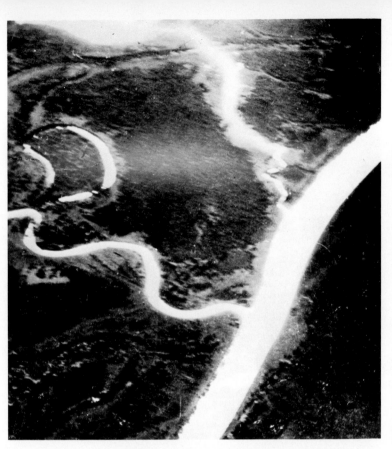

52-cm. mortar "Berta", saw acrion at Leningrad; French booty. The shell was 1.86 meters high and weighed 3,630 lbs. Range: 17.5 Kilometers. A soldier could fit easily into the barrel.

The Front: Everywhere
The Second World War obliterated borders between frontline and homeland. Bombing attacks turned the hinterland into war regions. (Right) German Gebirgsjäger on the slopes of a Kuban tributary 1943. ● Burning bomber after attack on a German air base.

A unique document is this color photo made by
Karl Knödler, showing the evacuation of the
Kuban bridgehead in the Fall of 1943. 200,000
soldiers, roughly 70,000 horses and 40,000
vehicles took passage through the strait of Kerch
to the Crimea.

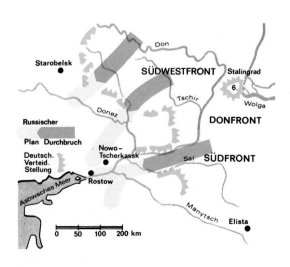

Starobelsk

Don

SÜDWESTFRONT

Stalingrad

6.

Tschir

Wolga

DONFRONT

Donez

Russischer
Plan Durchbruch

Deutsch.
Verteid.
Stellung

Nowo-
Tscherkassk

Sal

SÜDFRONT

Asowsches Meer

Rostow

Manytsch

Elista

0 50 100 200 km

Scenes of the Theaters of War
Kharkovs monumental buildings presented an unending temptation for the soldiers to take snapshots (Above). ● Rare photo of the traffic jam on the eastern shore of the Lower Bug; road of retreat, March 1944, for the 8th Army.

North of Lake Ilmen, and in front of Leningrad, the Spanish **Blue Division** erected its own monument of bravery. Here the 1st Battalion of the 269th I.D.
(*Operation Barbarossa* pages 150, 163, 289, 307, 326, 349 and *Scorched Earth*, pages 220-222).

They Marched at Our Side

The ideological tainted war breaks loose at the front. Vlassov threw in his lot for Germany against Stalin. Russian Cossack squadrons rode in field-grey, wearing the emblem of their country on their sleeves (Below). • Horthy's 2nd Hungarian Army fought on the Don (Upper right). • Vlassov Cossacks being trained as parts of the Wehrmacht (Center below). • Russian local volunteers wore an armband: "Working for the German Wehrmacht." • Designed by the Pétain government for the French volunteers, this medal for bravery cannot be worn in public; although it is still shown in the Military Museum in Paris. • (Center right) Leon Degrelle of the *Wallonian* Legion.

The Rumanians

Marschall Antonescu (Right) fought with two Armies against the Soviets. ● Rumanian units occupying Odessa (Above). ● Rumanian Corps in the Kuban bridgehead employed an unusual mode of traffic; Kerch was connected by a cable railway to the Crimea.

Battle Group of the 20th Panzer-grenadier Division in the Smolensk bend.

This photograph was taken south of Orel by
Erich Baür. A sector of "Operation Citadel", the
contest which Hitler promised should change
the fortunes of the war.

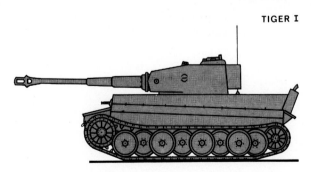

TIGER I

Fleet of Mercy
Airfields turned into immense bases for the wounded after days of intense fighting. Medical Ju 52's landed and started bringing the injured to main hospitals or special treatment centers in Germany. Russian paramedics worked side by side with German nurses and doctors. They were well educated and very able women (Above). Special suit cases contained their medical tools.

Above: In the hospital train. ● Below: Wounded officer with
tag. Red borders meant: "Unable to be transported."

A Tele-camera of Surveyor and Mapping Detachment 602; it was able to take landscape photos
with infra-red plates up to a distance of 80
kilometers.

Eye-piece View: 80 Kilometers
This rare war picture of the Caucasus region was taken by Alfred
Schwabe with a Leica camera coupled to a periscope while
working in the Surveyor and Mapping Detachment 602. To the
right: sector of the landscape.

Below: Panorama of Leningrad. In the center: Position Of
camera with orientation degrees. Numbers in meter give
distances from camera position.

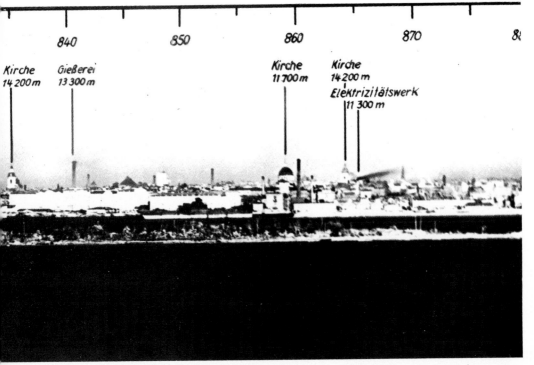

Assyr Su Basch
4349 m

Uschba
4691 m

Uliba
4369 m

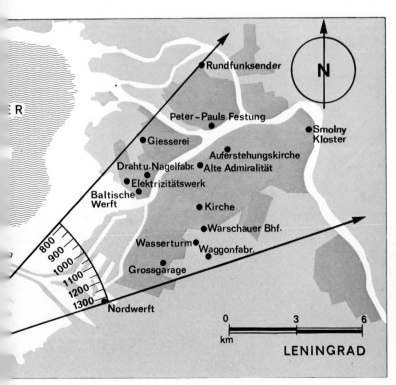

Rundfunksender

Peter-Pauls Festung

Smolny Kloster

Giesserei

Auferstehungskirche

Draht u. Nagelfabr.

Alte Admiralität

Elektrizitätswerk

Baltische Werft

Kirche

800
900
1000
1100
1200
1300

Warschauer Bhf.

Wasserturm

Waggonfabr.

Grossgarage

Nordwerft

0   3   6
km

LENINGRAD

1200

1210

Wasserturm des Warscha

12 800 m

260/261

Elbrus 5633 m Galakol 3424 m

Krasnodar
Noworossisk Maikop
Tuapse
Sotschi
Suchumi

K A U K A S U S

ELBRUS 5633 m
USCHBA 4691 m
DYCH–TAU 5198 m

Schwarzes

Meer

Kaspisch.

Meer

TIFLIS

T Ü R K E I

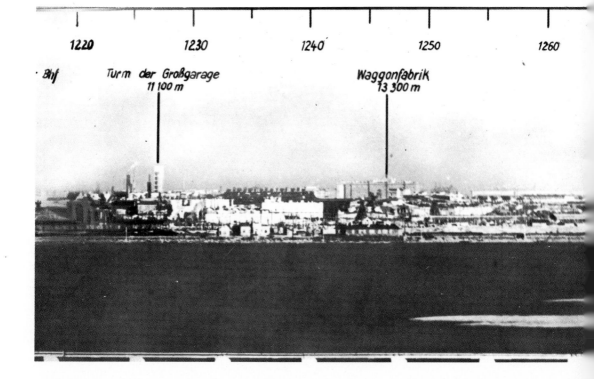

1220 1230 1240 1250 1260

· Bhf Turm der Großgarage
11 100 m

Waggonfabrik
13 300 m

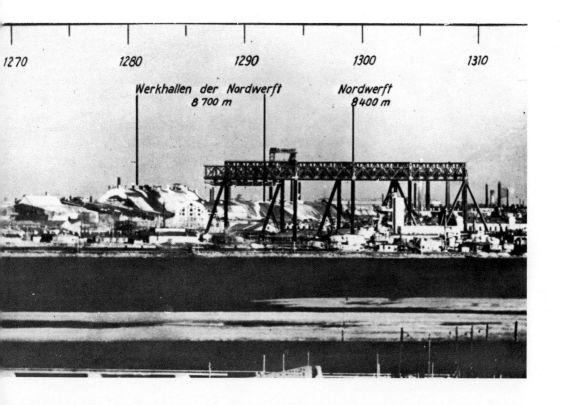

Werkhallen der Nordwerft
8 700 m

Nordwerft
8 400 m

**Elbrus-Leningrad:
2,500 Kilometer as the Crow Flies**
Left: German Gebirgsjäger moving up to
their positions. Mount Elbrus in the background. • The Soviets also had mountain
troops. Laying on the slopes of the high-
Caucasus, they kept the Germans from
taking the coastal roads. • Leningrad was
in the choke-hold of the German-Finnish
blockade. Defense Commissar Zhdanov
evacuated parts of the population over the
ice road of Lake Ladoga.

Phantoms of Lake Ilmen
This photo, transmitted to England in 1942, was supposed to be a secret weapon; scary and eerie looking, these self-propelled armored sleds, did not measure up to Russian expectations, just the contrary. These tanks on sleds did not do their jobs at all, and fell easy prey to the German defenses.

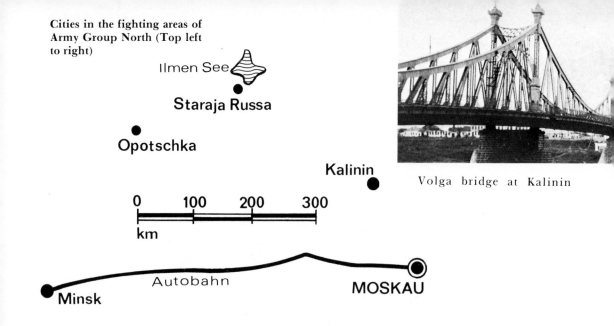

Ilmen See

Staraja Russa

Opotschka

Kalinin

0   100   200   300

km

Autobahn   **MOSKAU**

Minsk

Volga bridge at Kalinin

Staraya Russa

Cathedrals, market stalls

Factory section in Kalinin

Opotschka

Over the bridge

Main street
with Kremlin

Cornerstone Rzhev

At least 350,000 German soldiers knew the
Volga bridge of Rzhev (Above). *General* Model
held the city in the proximity of Moscow like a
break-water. Russian counter-attacks were
futile. About 30 Divisions of the 9th and 4th
Armies fought in the area. Especially severe
were the winter battles 1942/1943. (Top left)
Grenadiers counter attacking. (Below) Heavy
mortar firing at Soviet troop concentrations.
(Right) Preparations to blow the bridge.
(*Operation Barbarossa* pages 323-335 and
Scorched Earth, pages 238-247).

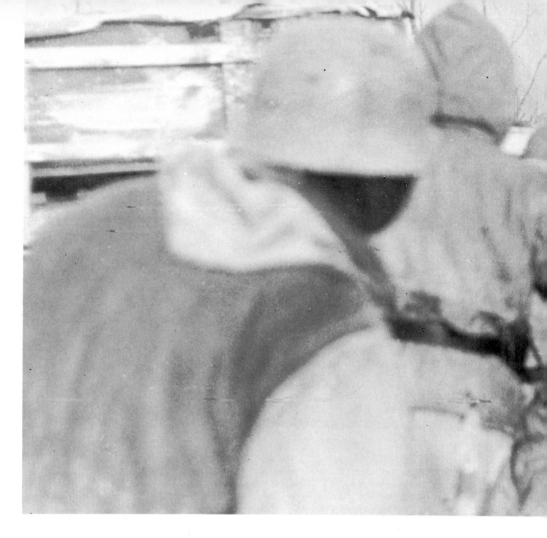

Cauldron of Demyansk

Supported by assault guns grenadiers advance and take enemy battle placements. ● A wounded Soviet Commander surrenders.
(*Operation Barbarossa*, pages 222-237).

Stronghold Velikiye Luki

Get ready to attack! 18th Panzer Detachment assembles for a relief thrust in January 1943 (Right). They break through and reach the surrounded fortress, driving through the famous arch of the citadel. ● But Russian artillery demolishes the vehicles. ● German riflemen and crews fight for more than 12 months to the bitter end. Only a few escaped. These photos were all taken by *Oberleutnant* Burg who died at Velikiye Luki.

(*Operation Barbarossa*, pages 247-259).

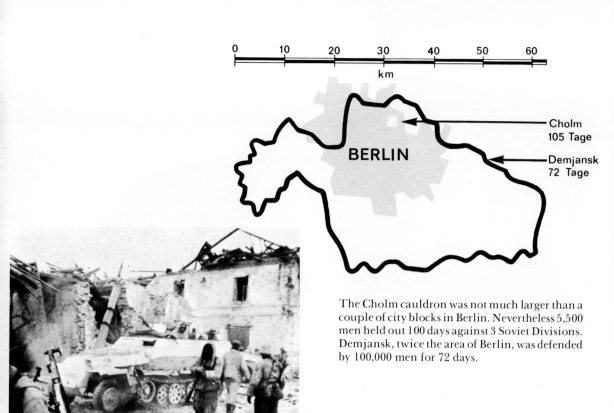

BERLIN

Cholm
105 Tage

Demjansk
72 Tage

The Cholm cauldron was not much larger than a couple of city blocks in Berlin. Nevertheless 5,500 men held out 100 days against 3 Soviet Divisions. Demjansk, twice the area of Berlin, was defended by 100,000 men for 72 days.

270/271

One Hundred Days of Encirclement at Cholm
Receiving his Knight's Cross, the Captain embraces his General expressing true friendship between men. It happened on March 20, 1942 in the cauldron of Cholm, when Captain Biecker received the decoration from General Scherer. Five weeks later, the Captain was killed at the ruins of the GPU building. ● The small encirclement was supplied by air. But collecting the dropped provision canisters under enemy fire often proved to be fatal.
(*Operation Barbarossa,* pages 357-360).

Dangerous Hunters
Snipers. Brave, very tricky, solitary fighters. Sometimes they laid fifty meters in front of their own lines, in excellent hideouts which they entered by night, and surveyed the opponents with their scopes. Carelessness resulted in a deadly shot, causing fear and insecurity among the enemy. ● The German sniper (Above) had 125 hits in fourteen days. ● Sniper Pavlutschenko, a Ukrainian girl, was decorated for her kills in the defense of Sevastopol.

South-east of Toropez

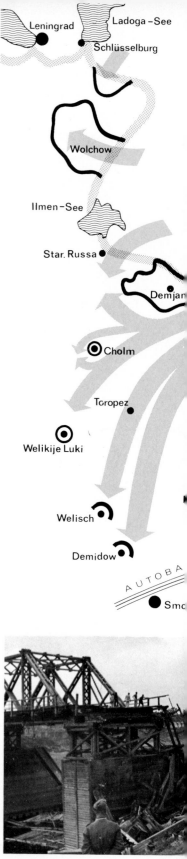

Cholm destroyed

The bridge of Velizh

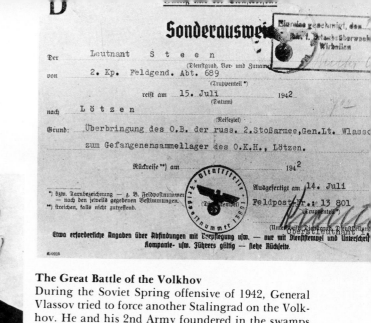

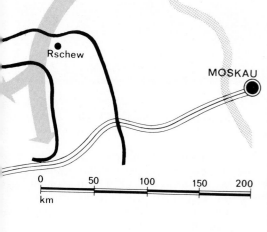

Seliger-See

Kalinin

Rschew

MOSKAU

0   50   100   150   200
km

The Great Battle of the Volkhov
During the Soviet Spring offensive of 1942, General Vlassov tried to force another Stalingrad on the Volkhov. He and his 2nd Army foundered in the swamps and woods; ultimately, he was captured. The catastrophe changed his attitude towards Stalin, and he defected to the Germans. After the war Vlassov was hanged in Moscow.
(*Operation Barbarossa*, pages 344-350 and 361-363).

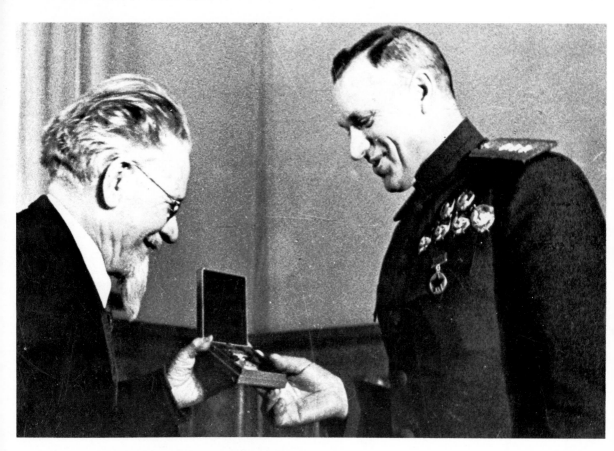

Ritterkreuz and Suvorov Medal
Unteroffizier Horst Naumann, a 21 years-old from Berlin, destroyed 21 Soviet tanks with his assault gun in the encirclement of Demyansk; six of them while attempting a decisive breakthrough. The first soldier of the Assault Artillery to receive the decoration, which General Höhne is awarding him. ● *Generaloberst* K. Rokossovsky gained his first merits defending Moscow, and in the battle of the Don front. Here he accepts the Suvorov Medal 1. Class from the President of the Supreme Soviet, M. Kalinin. ● Every soldier of the German Army could acquire the highest medals for bravery. The Red Army awarded decorations according to military rank. The Suvorov Medal 1. Class was for officers only.
(*Scorched Earth*, pages 228-229 and 291).

Burst Gun Barrel, Strictly prohibited to photograph a scene like this, Paul Stöcker took the photo at the 843rd Artillery Detachment, a reminder to the gunners, not only the danger from the enemy but that misfortune was waiting too. ● (Below) Firing positions of Heavy Artillery Detachment 740.

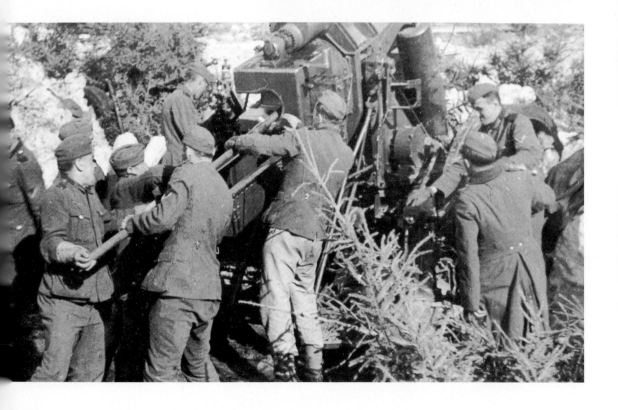

VI.
Caucasus, Kuban, Kerch
The Big Battle for Oil

When the armies of Army Group A set out
to take possession of the oilfields of the
Caucasus, 500 kilometers of steppe and one
of the mightiest mountain ranges lay ahead
of them. Infantry, Panzergrenadiers and
Gebirgsjäger fought along the age-old
highways of the Caucasus, the shore of the
Black Sea and the Kalmyk steppes. And
then, fighting their way back in bloody
combat. Some went to the north, but the
bulk into the Kuban bridgehead, from
there to the Crimea.

In the Land of the Circassians
Parching heat and pouring rain sees the Gebirgsjäger moving over the passes and through the valleys of the Caucasus. ● Pyatigorsk on the Kuma in the northern Caucasus, resembles a gold mining town of America.
(*Operation Barbarossa*, pages 443-457).

oad to Asia
he gleaming panorama of the Elbrus
ountains, is the background for the columns of
e 40th Panzer Corps driving through the
almyk steppes to the Terek. ● This was the last
bstacle before the oil region of Groznyy and the
ld Army road to Tiflis, Kutaissi and Baku was
ft behind on August 25, 1942. ● Supplies for the
nal thrust roll over the Terek bridge. But the
erman forces were not strong enough and
oviet resistance on the inclines of the Caucasus
n the vicinity of Ordchonikidse demonstrated its
ower (Left).
Operation Barbarossa, pages 472-475).

Edelweiss on Their Cap

Backbreaking labor by the Gebirgsjäger to bring the light Infantry gun into position at the Klukhor passage (Left). Despite the icy winds, men of the 1st and 4th Gebirgs Division climb the 5,633 meter high Mount Elbrus. After raising the flag, Andres Feldle took this photo of the group at the triangulation point. ● (Lower right) Gebirgsjäger on their way to their stations at the Laba valley. ● (Lower left) Scouts of a mounted Soviet Mountaineer Brigade on their tough panje ponies in the wooded Caucasus.
(*Operation Barbarossa*, pages 457-460).

Only the Cemeteries Remained
German Gebirgsjäger fought at heights of over
3,000 meters, took enemy positions while crossing
soaring rocky ridges, gale-lashed slopes and
precarious glaciers; positions nobody imagined
could be taken away by storm. The very last
objective the coast, proved to be impossible. The
Soviet counter offensive forced them to retreat
from the Caucasus.

The Last Yards to the Coast

Exits of the valleys into the coastal plains saw merciless defensive action by Soviet Marine units (Left). The sea and subtropical coastline were visible to German forces; the last kilometers were beyond their strength. ● The Russians were able to hold their positions north-west of Tuapse (Lower left). ● A few weeks later, the German withdrawal began. (*Operation Barbarossa*, pages 458-462 and *Scorched Earth*, pages 120-135).

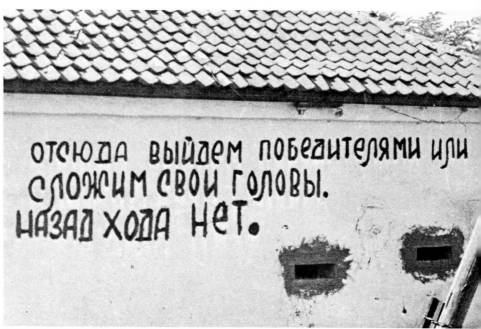

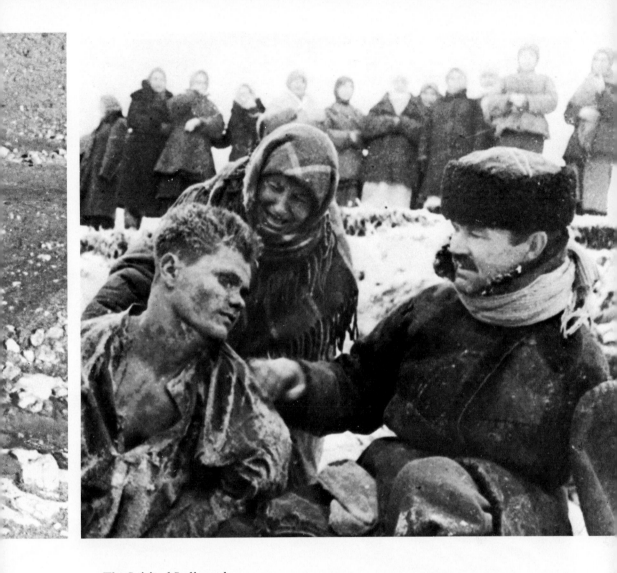

The Spirit of Stalingrad

At the end of 1942, the fanatical spirit of Stalingrad was awakened in the Caucasus. Native partisans knowing every valley and path, fought along the Ossetian Army road (Upper left). ● Walls of houses, turned into bunkers, in the town Ordschonikidse carried fighting slogans: "We'll finish here as victors or die; there is no more retreating." ● After the German withdrawal, the population searched for relatives. Parents find their son frozen to death at Pjatigorsk.

Route of Retreat

Dr. Hermann Schmidt and Toni Hupfloher took three photos, three scenes portraying the entire drama of withdrawal. ● (Left) Beaten, dead tired but still ready to fight. ● (Upper right) Two wounded men, resigned to their fate, wait at a battle station for help — or the end of their travels. ● Soviet low level fighters surprised German columns time and again.

292/293

The Volunteers

All countries of Europe mobilized volunteer movements against the Red Army. A train with French volunteers leaving Vernay. ● Arrival in Poland and still in French uniform. *Leutnant* Lovis and his platoon marching into the battle sector of the 7th I.D. ● The French suffered heavy casualties during the battle of Moscow.

March over the Sea
The sight of ice-bound boats and dune grasses
lets you breathe easier. They made it. The shore
of the Sea of Asov is reached. Parts of the 1st
Panzer Army had to march for 42 kilometers over
the frozen Sea of Asow to escape captivity. ●
Mission accomplished! The thirty day trek from
the Terek to the Don succeeded. A race against
weather and enemy.
(*Scorched Earth*, pages 124-125).

When Stalin Tried to Catch the 17th Army

The 17th Army was supposed to be cut off by an amphibian operation in the bay of Ozereyka February 1943. It ended in an appalling defeat for the Russians. Left on the beach of Ozereyka were destroyed Soviet tanks and landing craft of American origin (Left). ● The Red Army forced a bridgehead on Mount Myschkako (Below left). ● The final battle for Noworossisk began September 1943. The cement factory was the center of hot and heavy fighting (Below).
(*Scorched Earth*, pages 138-154).

Combat in the Kuban Bridgehead
A jump-off position into Asia, the bridgehead was held for eight months by 17th Army. A determined opponent ahead of them and the sea behind them. Infantry, Panzer crews and Gebirgsjäger units doubted their own ability to reach the Crimea, if the Russians broke through the Kerch highway. (Lower left) Disabled tanks of American origin before German lines.

300/301

Gültig für freie Urlaubsreisen auf kleinen Wehrmachtfahrschein | 160

... von ansteckenden
...kheiten.
...arzt und
...lungsarzt.

Kriegsurlaubsschein

Erholungsurlaub

Hauptmann Paul Stöcker
(Dienstgrad, Vor- und Zuname) ...umsteigebahnhof Wolkowysk

...n Einheit Feldp. No. 31 839 A
(Truppenteil) Abfahrt am 9. 6. 4... mit SF 74

...t vom .... 194..... bis einschl. .... 194 .... Uhr beurlaubt
Eintreffen am Gronau 3. Juli 1943

...ach G r o n a u (Westf.) nächster Bahnhof Gronau

...ach L i p p s t a d t (Westf.) nächster Bahnhof Lippstadt

...ach Westendorf (Tirol) nächster Bahnhof Westendorf

...r reist auf kleinen Wehrmachtfahrschein. Die Inanspruchnahme von Wehrmachtfahrkarten oder Fahrkarten
...es öffentlichen Verkehrs für die im Wehrmachtfahrschein bezeichnete Strecke ist verboten.

...eber die umstehenden Befehle ist er belehrt worden

URLAUBER-PLATZMARKE
Tag der Abfahrt des SF.-Zuges
vom Ausgangsbahnhof
SMOLENSK
8. Juni

Ausgefertigt am 6. Juni 194..

...inheit Feldp. No. 31 839
(Truppenteil)

Major und Abteilungskommandeur

E-Schein
Entlausungsschein

Der Inhaber dieser Bescheinigung

(Dienstgrad) (Name) (Feldpost-Nummer)

Entlausungsanstalt 65

2.Kol./Kw...

Between Smolensk and Westendorf
It was a long way from the company office, picking up ones leave papers, then off to the de-lousing station, and finally, laden with friends packages bound for home, to the train station and home to Frankfurt am Main. An entirely different trip is shown: 15th I.D. pulling out of La Rochelle, France straight to the frontline at Sinelnikovo early 1943; Break in Hanau for provisions. • Hot coffee in Terespol. (*Scorched Earth*, page 167).

End of furlough

304/305

To the Saving Shore

For months the men of *Generaloberst* Ruoff's 17th Army cast longing glances over to Kerch, the saving shore of the Crimea across the Taman peninsular. • End of September 1943 it finally happened: The Kuban bridgehead was being evacuated; engineers and navy transported the 17th Army to the Crimea (Bottom right). • An amphibious VW did dispatch duty between different landing zones. • Immense clouds over the blown up installations announced: The last troops have left the bridgehead.

VII.
"Operation Citadel"
"Panther" and "Tiger" Conjecture
for Change

Hitler's operation plan No. 6 ordered: "Every leader, every man, must be aware of the decisive importance of this attack." In directive No. 7 he decreed: "It must succeed under any circumstances; no carelessness or imprudence should give our intentions away." Time of attack and operational plans were already betrayed, but Hitler was unaware of it. The Red Army was well prepared, and lay waiting for the German divisions.

308/309

Moving Across the Country, Marching Over the Rivers
Sometimes Panzers, trucks and other vehicles of war were not to be seen for quite a while, and
so began the bad news, with the honored old parable: soldiers, comrades . . . again. ●
Beginning of 1943, *Feldmarschall* von Manstein stops the threatening Soviet offensive
between Donez and Dnjepr and fights the third battle for Kharkov. (Left) Wounded
combatants of the 19th Panzer Division, in the icy winter weather on their way to the field
hospital. ● (Above) The old Soviet foot bridge over the Dnieper at Dnepopetrovsk. Russians
carrying their wounded buddy to the western shore, into captivity.

Aces in the Summmer Battle
The supreme achievement of German Panzer construction
in the Second World War was the "Tiger", predator of
steel, and equipped with an 88-mm. gun. The official
terminology was Panzer VI. ● The "Eighty-eight" was
known to every Red Army or Tommy in Africa, and
proved to be an outstanding weapon in ground combat as
well as an anti-aircraft gun. ●
Armed with a 12.5-cm. cannon, the Soviet assault gun was
very dangerous, but ponderous; three rounds of the 88-mm.
knocked it out (Lower right). ● (Left) Panzer IV.

"The Italians are Blown Away"

These were the opening words of General Badanov's situation report for the 1st Guard Army Don, December 24, 1942. The Hungarian front sector of the Don collapsed. Penetrating the defense lines of the German Allies, the Russians directed their forces against the river Don, after their sweep of Stalingrad. Encirclements, chaos of resistance, disbandment (Above). ● Where is the enemy? A flare lights up the area. Russians hiding in the brush become visible. "Fire"! Tracers point the path of the machine gun rounds.

(*Operation Barbarossa*, page 538 and *Scorched Earth*, pages 104-110).

Kharkov, Four Times

Kharkov changed possession four times during the war. (Upper left) This unusual photo document taken in the summer battle of 1942 shows: a combination assault of tanks, airplanes and Cavalry. ● Force to withdraw from the city with his Waffen-SS troops in February, *Obergruppenführer* Hausser regained Kharkov in March 1943. ● The Russians return as victors to the hard suffering city of Kharkov August 1943.
(*Operation Barbarossa*, pages 155 and 270).

"Dora" to "Director"

One of the rare private photos of the Führer headquarters "Wolfsschanze", it shows *Feldmarschall* Keitel, *Reichsaussenminister* von Ribbentrop in front of Keitel's working quarters. (Above) ● Secured and camouflaged like no other field camp in the world, this establishment was situated in the deep woods near Rastenburg. The outer walls of the reinforced concrete bunkers were covered with a canopy of artificial leaves; the roofs planted with bushes and shrubs; Locating "Wolfsschanze" despite all of this security, top secrets still found their way into the Russian Army Communication Center. ● "Dora" to "Director"; two wireless messages intercepted from the agent "Dora", in Switzerland, to the "Director" in Moscow.

(*Operation Barbarossa*, page 90 and *Scorched Earth*, pages 82-101).

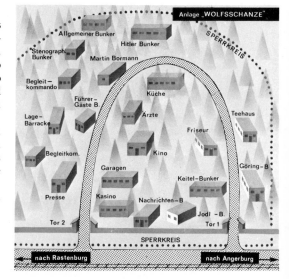

Anlage „WOLFSSCHANZE"

SPERRKREIS

Allgemeiner Bunker
Hitler Bunker
Stenograph. Bunker
Martin Bormann
Begleit-kommando
Küche
Führer–Gäste B.
Arzte
Teehaus
Lage-Barracke
Friseur
Begleitkom.
Kino
Göring-B
Garagen
Keitel-Bunker
Presse
Kasino
Nachrichten–B
Jodl –B.
Tor 2
Tor 1
SPERRKREIS
nach Rastenburg
nach Angerburg

10.6.43
----

dora an direktor: von werther, 4.6. ... im bereich der 2. armee
und 4.armee in vollzug begriffene bewegungen der zum angriff
auf kursk bereitgestellten motorisierten truppen wurden am 28.
mai ploetzlich auf befehl mansteins rueckgaengig gemacht. ...

12.6.1943
----

direktor an dora: geben sie an lucie auftrag, durch mitarbeiter
sofort festzustellen alle angaben ueber schwere panzer, genannt
panther.
wichtig ist:
1. konstruktion dieses panzers und technische charakteristik
2. konstruktion seiner panzerung
3. einrichtung des feuerwerfers und fuer vernebelung
4. standorte der betriebe, welche diesen panzer produzieren,
   und wie hoch ist die produktion monatlich?

"Best Units, Best Weapons"

Thus ordered Hitler, for the battle of Kursk. "Tigers" roll to the front. • "Goliath", a miniature Panzer was ready. • "Panther", the new battle Panzer with a high velocity 7.5-cm. long barreled cannon on which Hitler placed high hopes. • Faithful old rifle-cups for rifle grenades were mass produced. *Oberst* Rudel, the most successful tank destroyer from the air, had his Ju 87G equipped with an anti-tank cannon. • The trump card was the rolling artillery bunker, "Tiger Ferdinand." Named for its constructor Ferdinand Porsche. Another one of a special kind: Heavy Tank Destroyer with a 12.8-cm. gun (Bottom right).

of a special kind: Heavy Tank Destroyer with a 12.8-cm. gun (Bottom right).

318/319

Ausstattung „Zitadelle" für Nordgruppe (9. Armee)		
Verpflegung. 10 Tagessätze 266 000 Mann	5 320 t 266 Güterwagen	
Munition.	12 300 t 615 Güterwagen	
Futter. für 50 000 Pferde	6 000 t 300 Güterwagen	
Betriebsstoff.	11 182 cbm 82 Betr.st.Züge	

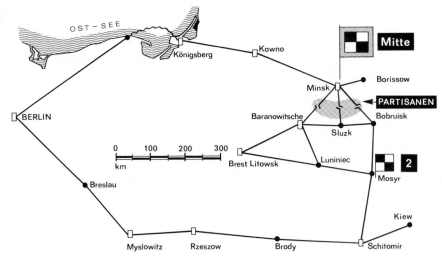

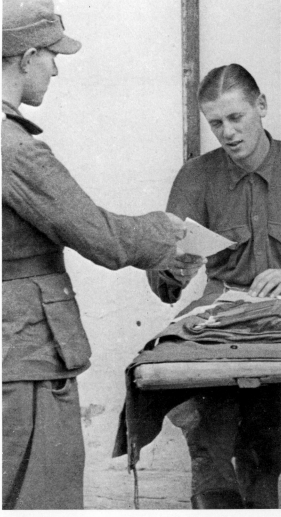

Communication connections between Army Group Center and 2nd Army passed through country occupied by partisans and suffered continuous interruptions. Since the partisans could not be totally eliminated, General Praun directed that 300 kilometers of hook up be strung to the outskirt the Partisan problem. An excellent effort — but at what costs (Right page)

Knowledge is power

The brain of war is the Center of Communications, prime cell of every military undertaking; base of situation reports, operational plans, directions, orders. Reason enough to make intelligence departments a decisive arm of any army. ● (Left) Searching for a jam in the wiring of a reconnaissance echelon. How far was the withdrawal of the troops? Where are the rear guards? Where is the enemy? Questions that decided survival of Armies. Wireless messages and long distance calls reached the Commanding officer of a communications center (Middle). To find a solution in difficult times, the Army Commander had to have exact information. (Right) *Generaloberst* von Weichs, Supreme Commander of Army Group B.

Wireless Station and Dispatch Rider

Connection to Command Posts for help, orders, advice and recommendations, meant the presence of a wireless station. ● (Above) Link between troops and staff in the main battle line, was the portable wireless, (Right-transmitter; Left receiver with battery). ● Listening-troops waged war of a different kind. Induction or direct tapping of enemy telephone lines was their way to eavesdrop. Many military achievements were the results of their work (Center). ● When all wires were down, and the wireless jammed, then, only the old fashioned dispatch rider could help. (*Scorched Earth*, pages 169-174).

322/323

Bombs and Shells

Tremendous artillery barrages opened every battle. ● (Right) Heavy German mortar. ● (Below) Soviet field piece. The Russians were masters of artillery fighting. "Artillery is the queen of armament" as cited by Stalin. ● Aerial bombs SD 1 and SD 2, developed by the Germans, were containers filled with 180 or 360 one or two Kilogram bombs to put massed Soviet artillery positions and blocks of anti-tank guns out of action. Opening close to the ground, these high explosive mini bombs were dropped into enemy sites. The effects were devastating.

324/325

Medic! Medic!
The plaintive cry sounding over the battle grounds
signaled the work for the medics to begin. Giving
first aid in the fire zone, the wounded were brought
back to a sheltered area. The field hospital was the
next station. From there to a collecting unit, which
provided improvised or organized transportation to
the main dressing stations.

Orel ●

⬇

Olchowatka ●   Zentralfront

Kursk ●

                         Woroneschfront

Obojan ●
         ⬆

Bjelgorod ●   Steppenfront

Charkow ●

                         Südwestfront

0   100   200   km

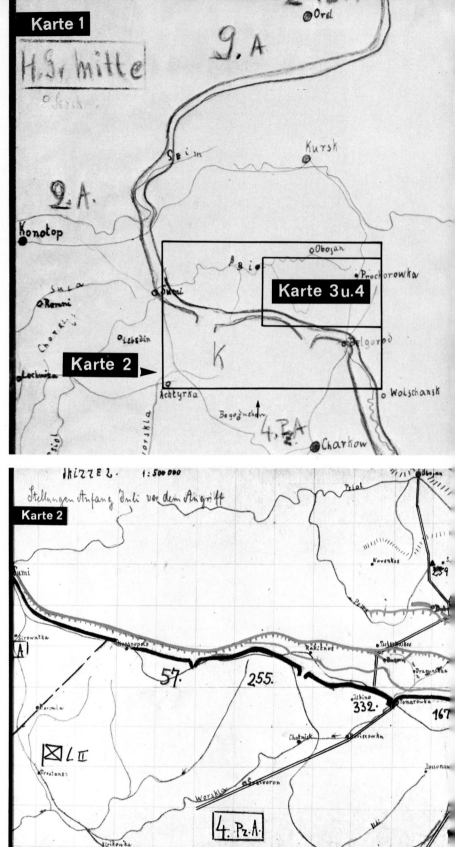

Karte 1

H.Gr. Mitte

O Sensk

9. A.

○ Orel

Seim

Kursk ●

2. A.

Konotop ●

Ssula   Psiol

○ Romni

Chorol

○ Lebedin

○ Lochwiza

Ssumi

Karte 3 u. 4

○ Obojan

● Prochorowka

○ Bjelgorod

Karte 2 ➤

K

Achtyrka

Worskla

○ Wolschansk

Bogoduchow

4. Pz.A.

Charkow ●

SKIZZE.   1:500 000

Stellungen Anfang Juli vor dem Angriff

Karte 2

Psiol   ○ Obojan

Nowenkoe   2. S. 9

Ssumi

Peel

Sirowatka   Krassnopole   Rakitnoe   Tscherkasskoe

○ Butowo   ○ Dragunska

57.   255.   Ilbino   Tomarowka   167

332.

⊠ L II   Chotmisk ← Borissowka

○ Trostanez   ○ Bessonow

Worskla   Strawoon

○ Trikowka   4. Pz.-A.

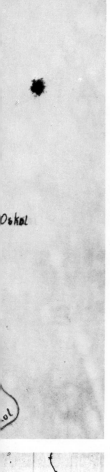

Decision in the East

Trying to settle the loss of Stalingrad and regain the initiative was Hitler's plan for the battle of Kursk during the summer of 1943. His gamble failed. Published for the first time, these hand drawn sketches by the Commander-in Chief of the 4th Panzer Army, *Generaloberst* Hoth (Upper left) show a very sober and objective view of the battle progress. ● The Russian counterpart, General Rokossovskiy (Above with map) visited with his staff in a northern sector shortly before the German assault. (lower right) City of Byelgorod, the pivot point of 4th Panzer Army and Army Detachment Kempf.
(*Scorched Earth*, pages 3-81).

Danger! Mines!
Very dangerous business was the clearing of mines before combat. Lanes for infantry and Panzers had to be provided for, using electronic equipment or by simply probing the ground with the bayonet — find the devil's eggs. (Lower left) Soviets clearing German tank mines. (Right) Germans digging for Soviet box mines.
(*Scorched Earth*, pages 21-22).

330/331

"Tigers" are Coming

Characteristic picture of the war in Russia 1943/1944: Heavy Panzers, rolling fortresses cleared the way for the combat groups. (Above) *Feldwebel* Strippel was one of the most successful Panzer commanders. Serving in the 1st Panzer Division, 70 kills earned him the Knight's Cross with Oak Leaves. (Lower right) Pilots threw out message-cannisters with important observations or developments for their troops on the battlefield. The cannister would release smoke so that it could be easily located.
(*Scorched Earth*, page 58).

334/335

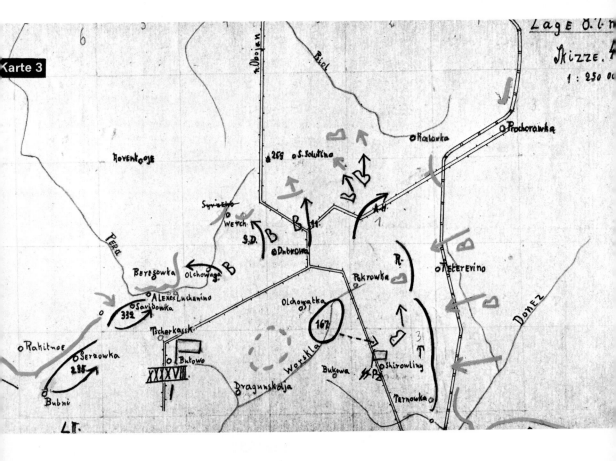

Panzers to the Front

This was the classic order of the second world war. Mobile fighting machines replaced the cavalry charges of past battles. Panzer assault meant absolute action. Direct hit on a T-34 at a distance of 2,000 meters, as seen from the gunner of a "Tiger Ferdinand." He set the firing angle with the pointers of the optic. Orders given in a neighboring Panzer: "Turret at 3 o'clock, enemy tank, fire at will!" ● The infantry take cover and an 88mm starts barking at once. ● And the T-34 across the way caught it. ● Battle situation as seen in Hoth sketch on the afternoon of July 8, in the southern sector. ● The leader opponent in this sector was the brave and talented Army Commander Vatutin. ● German jump-off positions at Belgorod were no secret to Russian air reconnaissance; their photos were extremely accurate.

Decisive phase of "Operation Citadel"
Grenadiers mounted on Panzers drive through
the pouring rain for a last attempt to break
through the Soviet front line at Oboyan. ●
July 12 and the Russians move their reserves
(map). Counter attacks and deeply echeloned
anti-tank positions, stop the German onslaught (right). Artillery observer in the tree.
Field Artillery in the open gives support to the
Russian attack.

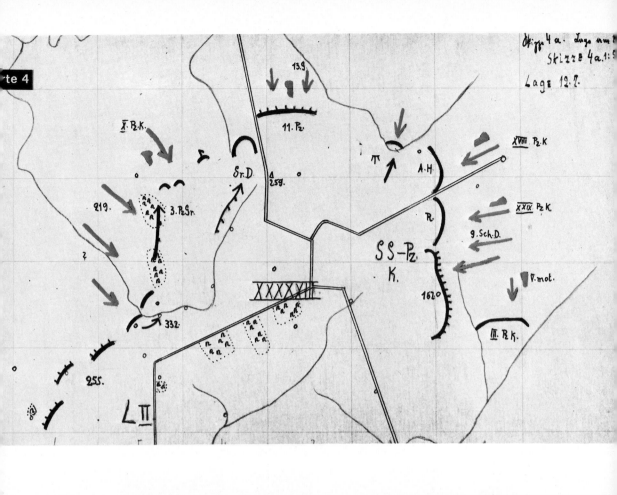

The Stage - Means Everything

Entertainment and relaxation was needed by millions of soldiers in the true sense of the word. There were variety shows. There was cabaret. Places for Operetta or the more demanding Opera. (Lower left) A widely known Cabaret in Kharkov was "Panzersprenggranate" ("The Anti-Tank Shell"). ● City theatre Poltavas handbill announced "The Gypsy Baron." Director Paul Wölffer presented Russian artists. The following double-page photo shows part of "Musical Mosaic", taken from the parquet by Dr. Ott.

Missing in Action
One of the dancers of the Vitebsk Front Theatre Ballet lost a leg during a bomb attack on Berlin, but kept performing with an artificial lower leg. A story celebrated by the Landser in a big way. Truth? Or one of those legends grown exclusively in soldiers circles? Warranted fact is the Theatre and Ballet Troupe disappeared — missing in action. So read the official report. Perished fatalities of the bloody summer battles for "Fortress Vitebsk" where they stayed to the end.

Partisans

Partisan war, fourth front, born out of the Second World War. Complicated military and moral problems followed, defending against the combative partisans. ● (Above) Taking the oath from Soviet instructors. ● (Top right) A few minutes ago still an ordinary peasant standing by the way. ● Entire German divisions and heavy weapons were needed for the fight in the Hinterland. Their use on the front would have been much more important. Both sides, partisans and defenders were very tricky: if the booby-trapped telephone pole was cut, the partisan never survived the explosion. This became well known, and was a powerful deterrent.

7m

◀ **Abreisszünder**

◀ **Sprengpatrone**

2m

Khrushchev's Idea: Dig in the Tanks

Against the order of Stalin, at the zenith of the battle of Kursk, Khrushchev had all tanks dug in to form an irresistible anti-tank front. Lower left) This defense stopped the last German assault. Flames from blown up tanks and glowing shell fragments paint a surrealistic picture of the Panzer duels at Prokhorovka. • (lower right) Soviet 12-cm. mortar was a dreaded weapon. The Red Army was lavishly equipped with the "Cannon of the Infantry"; not so the Germans. Soviet propaganda used this to the limit by saying: Every second German soldier has the Iron Cross; every second Red soldier has a mortar.

(*Scorched Earth*, pages 52-74).

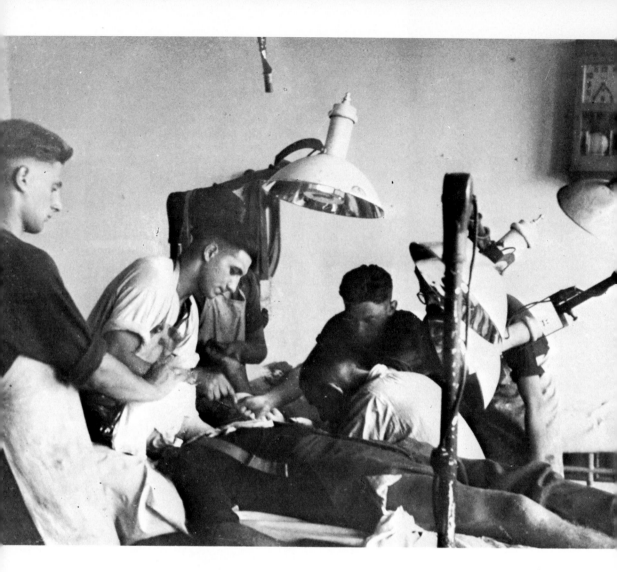

Occurrence in Akhtyrka

For the Germans 34,000 wounded and 7,000 dead
during twelve days of battle at Kursk was the cost.
Located in a school on the outskirts of Akhtyrka was a
hospital. Surgeons worked feverishly (Above). All the
doctors were killed by a direct bomb hit four hours after
this photo was taken. • They were buried in a soldier's
cemetery. Bodies in the mass grave were covered with
sand and brushwood. • Three days later, the battle of
Kursk was lost. The Russians came. Not to reveal any
information to the enemy, the Germans leveled their
graves to conceal them.

346/347

The Battle is Lost
The face of the German soldier now looks different than it did during 1941 or 1942. ● Now the Russian photos show the conquered battlefields covered with dead Germans. ● The chaos of retreat is reflected in German pictures. ● In the Soviet training camps, the banners carry proud slogans: "The Red Army threw the Germans 600-700 kilometers back to the west."

В ЗИМНЕЕ НАСТУПЛЕНИЕ КРАСНАЯ АРМИЯ УНИЧТОЖИЛА 2 ОТ[БОР]НЫЕ ФАШИСТСКИЕ АРМИИ ПОД СТАЛИНГРАДОМ, РАЗБИЛА И ПЛЕНИЛА РУМЫ[Н]СКУЮ, ИТАЛЬЯНСКУЮ И ВЕНГЕРСКУЮ АРМИИ, ОТБРОСИЛА НЕМЦЕВ НА 600 - 700 КИЛОМЕТРОВ НА ЗАПАД.

VIII.
"Scorched Earth"
350/351   **Retreat to the Dnieper**

The fourth battle for Kharkov began late in the summer of 1943. The Donets metropolis was evacuated by Manstein. That his assumption was correct is proven by four sets of numbers: Fall 1943 — Army Group South consisted of 60 Divisions with 720,000 men. The same front sector contained 264 Soviet Divisions with 1,700,000 men. Only a timely withdrawal behind the wide Dnieper gave the Germans a chance for effective defense. Hitler, in this case agreed. To deny the Russians any kind of reserves in the abandoned land, burn and destroy everything of use or value: "Scorched Earth."

Highway for Horses and Pigs
To the west towards the Dnieper past burnt barns and demolished factories, went the drive of horses, pigs, cattle and sheep. ● Clouds of dust from the unending treks darkened the sun and at the same time, 3,000 trains carried the live inventory of a 300 kilometer wide strip from the region between Stalino and Kiev. After the last railway car passed the main-rails and trunk lines were blown.
(*Scorched Earth*, page 294).

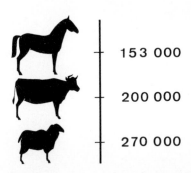

153 000

200 000

270 000

Migration of Spectres
The civilians traveled on horseback, on carts and carriages or walked along with the German divisions to the safety of the Dnieper. Like prehistoric clans, women and children moved into their nightly compounds. ● Despairing and perplexed many of them waited in demolished narrow-gauge railroad stations. For what?

354/355

Savior Dnieper

This mighty river was supposed to become the "Eastern Wall" and its cities, fortresses against the Red Army. ● (Second row left) Duisburg of the Soviet Union, Dnepropetrovsk. (Right side) Blasted bridge of Kremenchug. ● Energy center of the Western Ukraine, the dam of Zaporozhye. Hitler ordered six Divisions and one Panzer regiment into the city. But the Russians attacked with forces ten times stronger. ● (lower row, left to right) General von Mackensen at the dam site. Loading the explosive charges on October 14. ● The dam is blasted during the night of the fifteenth.

(*Scorched Earth*, pages 331-336).

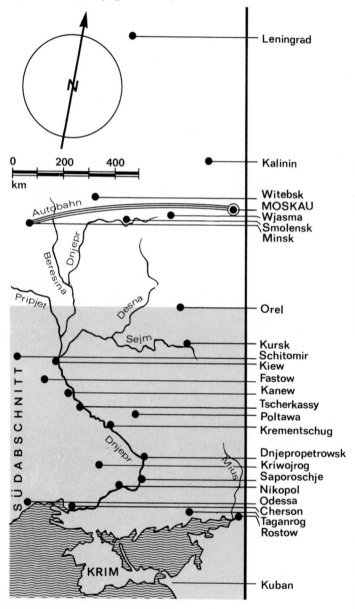

Leningrad

0 200 400
km

Kalinin

Autobahn

Witebsk
MOSKAU
Wjasma
Smolensk
Minsk

Dnjepr
Beresina

Pripjet

Desna

Orel

Sejm

Kursk
Schitomir
Kiew
Fastow
Kanew
Tscherkassy
Poltawa
Krementschug

Dnjepr

Mius

Dnjepropetrowsk
Kriwojrog
Saporoschje
Nikopol
Odessa
Cherson
Taganrog
Rostow

SÜDABSCHNITT

KRIM

Kuban

Photographed at Kischinev on the Dneister, daring shock troops secured the bridges against partisans and commando groups.

Stadttheater Poltawa

Der Zigeunerbaron

Operette in drei Akten von Johann Strauss

Personen:

Graf Homonay, Husar . . . . Nikolaj Wlassow
Sandor Barinkay . . . . Nikolaj Maschenko
Zsupan, Shweinezüchter . . Konstantin Schwedow
Arsena, seine Tochter . . . . Euphrosinia Nossowa
Mirabella, Arsenas Erzieherin . . Helene Borisowa
Ottokar, ihr Sohn . . . . Wassili Tarassow
Canero, Advokat . . . . Iwan Lasorenko
Czipra, alte Zigeunerin . . . . . Tamara Nikolenko
Saffi, ihre Tochter . . . . Violetta Bagmet
Pali, Zigeuner . . . . Jakow Kladowij

Im zweiten Akt: Ballett-Einlage
(nach der II. Ungarischen Rhapsodie von Franz Liszt)

Pause nach dem I. und II. Akt

Musikalische Leitung: Hermann Schjukowski
Bühnenbilder: Leonid Reprinzew
Choreinstudierung: Pawel Schapowalenko
Ballettmeister: Juro Kusmenko
Inszenierung: Obergefr. Siegfried Paul Wölffer

Vitebsk
White Russia's old district capital panorama
suggested a stage setting. A lively Theatre life
flourished. Among the guests were many stars
and groups of comedians.

Fighting is Only Part of a War
Marching, working and suffering are the other parts. ● Ambulances got stuck across a small river (Above). ● Passing them, the chief of an artillery battery scouts the area for a firing position.

Symbol of the great Dneiper bend: The district
church of Kremenchug stayed untouched.

Pripjet

Desna

ZENTRALFRONT

WORONESCHFRONT

Kiew

Achtyrka

Charkow

STEPPENFRONT

Winniza

Kanew
Tscherkassy

Krementschug

SÜDWESTFRONT

15. Sep.
ooooooo
30. Sep.

Dnjepropetrowsk

Stalino

Deutsch   Russisch

Saporoschje

SÜDFRONT

Nikopol

Taganrog

0   100   200

km

Wotan-
stellung

Dnjepr

Cherson

Melitopol

Odessa

ASOWSCHES
MEER

SCHWARZES MEER

KRIM

Scorched Earth
After sacrificing enormous stretches of country to the
German Blitz, Stalins order of July 3, 1941, decreed: "If
you are unable to transport it, destroy it." Forced to
retreat to the Dneiper by the Russians in 1943, Hitler
ordered the same: "Every village must be burnt." And
the hapless country burns (Below).
(*Scorched Earth*, pages 289-297).

Bread
A White Russian woman cutting her bread — an eternally stirring gesture — photographed by Alfred Tritschler. ● This snapshot of a young Ukranian girl from Stalino at her open-air baking oven, was taken by Herbert Kuntz.

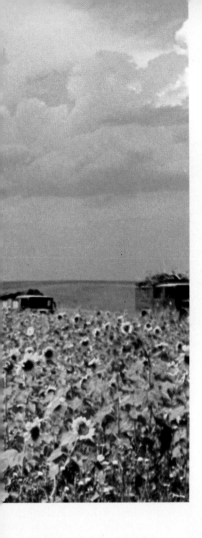

Seen from afar, a field of sunflowers had the effect
of a glittering ocean. ● Hungarian cavalry.

(Above) Southern tip of the Crimea, harbor and fortress Balaklava, after being taken in November 1941. ● (Left) Overhanging glacier at the Chotyou-Tau pass in the Elbrus region. A hazardous path, the Russians lurked below.

9th company Panzer-grenadier *Grossdeutschland*
buries their fallen comrades in Borosovka. Here
they still had coffins and crosses. Lots of crosses;
because of overwhelming enemy forces and the
unrealistic holding strategy of Hitler overtaxed
the troops.

Fight for the River
Medical company of Panzer-grenadier Regiment
3 crosses the river at Cherkassy. ● Sustaining
bridgeheads were defended by assault guns
against enemy tank thrusts.

Submerged Bridges and Paratroop Landings
Trying to cross the Dnieper ahead of the Germans the Russians used any methods available to them. Sunken foot bridges were almost invisible. ● Guards of commando groups used one-man boats to ford the river. ● To collapse the Dnieper defense, Soviet Supreme Command dropped three Paratroop Brigades behind the German front line (Below). ● (Upper right) General Nehring's 24th Panzer Corps smashed the full scale Soviet airborne operation at Bukrin.

Tanks, Tanks, Tanks
No strategy or bravery helped: At the end of 1943 the
worn out German units were no match for Soviet
supremacy of men and weaponry. Powerful tank
thrusts charged the Dnieper bridgeheads (Left). ●
The German Grenadiers fought for their lives.
(Above) ● They had no Panzers left, the tanks were
either lost during the retreat, or had to be destroyed
for lack of fuel. Instead of mot., it was "hot" (horse
trot) (Below).

Backyard of the Front

The term "Collection Staff" scared every man
returning from furlough. It meant being taken away
from the train, into a scraped together outfit and
sent to the lousiest sector of the front. • Standing in
line to be registered with people one had never seen
before. Then into the boxcars with officers and
sergeants whose names you had never heard before.
• And again, waiting along some wall for orders. It
happened to Erich Andres who photographed it.

ПРОЛЕТАРИИ ВСЕХ СТРАН, СОЕДИНЯЙТЕСЬ!
PROLETARIER ALLER LÄNDER, VEREINIGT EUCH!

ВСЕСОЮЗНАЯ
КОММУНИСТИЧЕСКАЯ
ПАРТИЯ (б)
СЕКЦИЯ КОММУНИСТИЧЕСКОГО
ИНТЕРНАЦИОНАЛА

KOMMUNISTISCHE
PARTEI (B)
DER SOWJET-UNION
SEKTION DER KOMMUNISTISCHEN
INTERNATIONALE

ЦК. ВКП (б)

ВСЕСОЮЗНАЯ
КОММУНИСТИЧЕСКАЯ ПАРТИЯ
(БОЛЬШЕВИКОВ)
Пролетарии всех стран, соединяйтесь!

ПАРТИЙНЫЙ БИЛЕТ

№ 1705136 ✳

Фамилия *Кобзев*

Имя и отчество *Андрей Петрович*

Год рождения *1907*

Время вступления в партию *февраль 1938 г.*

Наименование организации, выдавшей билет *Пер-
новский кантком Немреспублики*

Личная подпись *Кобзев* —

М. П.

Секретарь Райкома

А. Несынов

9 августа 1938 г.

KOMMUNISTISCHE PARTEI (Bolschewiki)
DER SOWJET-UNION
Proletarier aller Länder, vereinigt euch!

PARTEIMITGLIEDSBUCH

№ 1705136 ✳

Familienname *Kobsew*

Vor- und Vatersname *Andrej Petrowitsch*

Geburtsjahr *1907*

Datum des Eintritts in die Partei *Fewral 1938 g.*

Benennung der Organisation, die das Mitgliedsbuch
ausgestellt hat *Pernowskaer Kantkom
d. ASSR d. Wolgadeutschen*

Eigenhändige Unterschrift *Kobsew* —

Pl. f. St.

Sekretär des Raykoms

A. Nesynow

„9„ *August* 1938 g.

10

On the Mius

Mariupol, the Russian Bochum on the Sea of Asov, with its forges, rolling mills, docks and warehouses, lies two thousand kilometers from the German heavy industrial Ruhr area. The men of the newly restored 6th Army fought a tremendous battle in the fall of 1943: 31,133 Germans in opposition to 136,500 Russians; seven Panzers against 165 Soviet Tanks. The murderous deficit is reflected in the faces of the combatants of the 29th Corps. (*Scorched Earth*, pages 279-284).

It was Khrushchev's Victory
Nikita Sergeyivitsch Khrushchev ordered on November 1,1943: "No matter the costs, Kiev must fall on the anniversary of the October Revolution." (Left) Two thousand guns, and five hundred "Stalin Organs", hammered the city on November 3rd ● (Above) Even during a German air attack Russian combat engineers keep building their bridge. The sign carries the inscription: Kiew. ● The city falls on November 6. Using dogs, the engineers look for hidden German mines. ● "Comrade General, how long will the war last"?
(*Scorched Earth*, pages 324-327).

The Fourth Front
47% of its ground covered by forests, makes the Soviet Union the most
wooded country in the world. The secret of the victorious partisan war.
● To fight them, employment of heavy weapons — here "Nashörn
(Rhinoceros)" — was a must. ● Cornered the partisans fought
furiously. ● (Above) Ic of the 40th Panzer Corps, Major Kandutsch
greets one of the most effective partisan hunters, Major Abuschinow of
a Kalmyk Detachment; in the center the German *Wachtmeister*
(Cavalry Sergeant) Willi Lilienthal.

Russian Children Along the Road

Photos of children taken close to the front lines, and in the rear, by Carl Heinrich. ● The last picture is Russian showing the teacher instructing her class in front of their demolished school in Leningrad. ● "Children along the road" had to be the title for these photos. They let you feel that the children were real, the innocent sacrifices of a passing war — even if they didn't understand it at all.

390/391

Counterstroke
Photos of an important operation: The German counter attack in November 1943, stopped the Russian tempest to the west of Kiev with a few divisions. Even Zhitomir with its huge supply depots was taken back by the 48th Panzer Corps. ● (Lower right) Previous to the attack by the 7th Panzer Division, directives were given. Divisional Commander General von Manteuffel (left) holder of the Knight's Cross with Diamonds, *Oberst* Schulz (center) and *Oberst* von Steinkeller (with cane). ● Panzers and Grenadiers of the 1st Panzer Division broke the last resistance in the city. (*Scorched Earth*, pages 328-331).

Time Stands Still
Drizzling rain. Grey in grey. Stench of cordite in the air. The two Russian cavalry-men tried to escape. It happened west of Tula, the city of silversmiths. This eery picture is one of the best war photos taken by Gerhard Tietz.

Only the Uniform . . .
Both pictures show the officer corps a German Panzer-grenadier regiment, and the participants of a Soviet officers instruction course, during spring 1942. 15 of the 45 Germans fell, 2 were missing in action and 19 were wounded. Only 9 men survived the war unharmed. ● The numbers of the Russians are unknown but they could hardly be any lower. ● (Top right) German *Oberleutnant* and Russian *Oberstleutnant* — the difference: only the uniforms.

1939: Baden-Würtemberg 35th Infantry Division

IX.
The Front Collapses
Only Graves Remained

The Russians broke through at Kirovograd and surrounded four German Divisions. They escaped by a very narrow margin. Then came Cherkassy; encirclement of the 1st Panzer Army in the headlands of the Carpathians. And the catastrophe of the Crimea. Finally, in the summer of 1944, it hit Army Group Center: the Berezina became the German Cannae. The Red Army stormed to the Vistula and to the borders of East Prussia.

400/401

Russian Tank Wave Rolls

Soviet tank brigades storm out of many Dnieper bridgeheads in November 1943
(Lower right). Their trains, clearly visible, move to the west. ● Trying to hinder the
Russian advance, the Germans make use of every available method. (Upper
left)Destroyed tracks seen in this Russian photo. ● (Lower left) shows the German
picture of a "Railwolf." ● One of the best Soviet tank leaders in these weeks was
General Katukov, Supreme Commander of the 1st Guards Tank Army; (Above) the
photo was taken 1941.

Do You Have Mail for Me?

How many times did a soldier ask that question at mail call? Some men never received anything, but they still stood there everytime. ● During the time of encirclements and breaking defenses, when the trains always got stuck somewhere, the Landser (GI) became deeply frustrated. No mail meant imminent catastrophe.

Quagmire
January/February 1944, and the 24th Panzer Division moved in anguish from one battlefield to the other: From Nikopol 300 kilometers to the north. But, they were called back without firing a shot. Another one of Hitler's senseless edicts. The Division, ready for combat moved for weeks over muddy roads while the tragedy befell Korsun and Nikopol. ● (Left) Commander of the 24th Panzer Division, General von Edelsheim.
(*Scorched Earth*, pages 362-363).

Cherkassy - Tragedy for Six Divisions

Holding out after twenty days of being surrounded. 3rd Panzer Corps came close for the relief. Breakout! On February 16, 1944 they had their last warm meal in the cauldron (Above). Then they move out . . . Towards the rescuers. ● They are progressing from the west — here parts of the 1st Panzer Division (Upper right). ● Leading his heavy Panzer Regiment Dr. Franz Bäke (Field cap and oak leaves). Only ten kilometers divide them. ● But Soviet tanks waiting on the governing heights barred them from saving the bridge over the Gniloy Tikitich. One who made it was *Oberst* Franz (visored cap). (Lower right) Russian victors and the signs of German defeat. (*Scorched Earth*, pages 256-385).

The Ladle - Best Loved Weapon of All
How similar the photos! Field kitchen and ladle
were the most cherished institutions for soldiers on
both sides. • Russian sergeants preferred the German
mess kits.

The Rolling Hube-cauldron

"I still have a can of meat, Captain." It turned into dinner at the mud covered cart of the 2nd Company. (Above) ● 1st Panzer Army left the cauldron of Kamenets-Podolskiy like a wandering hedgehog. They forded four rivers. Punched through two enemy Armies. Provisions from supply canisters by air (Upper right foreground empty canister with chute). ● Motorcycle and car were replaced by the Panye horse: a piece of field cable for stirrups, rope for reins. Who would have recognized the men of the 1st East Prussian I.D., proven veterans in hundreds of battles? ● Marshal Schukow was willing to deal the 200,000 men of the 1st Panzer Army the fate of Stalingrad. But General Hube had some entirely different ideas. (*Scorched Earth*, pages 386-404).

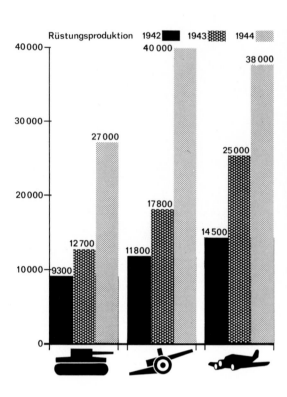

Rüstungsproduktion 1942 ■ 1943 ▨ 1944 ▨

40 000

40 000

38 000

30 000

27 000

25 000

20 000

17 800

14 500

12 700

11 800

10 000 9300

0

Modern war consists of 10% fighting and 90% working. The field army of 1870 required only farriers. Repair workshops of the last war played a role which could win or loose a battle. The front stood still without their labor (Statistic below) the same as without armament production of the homeland. One of the miracles of the last war was the rising output of weaponry despite the hail storm of bombs. ● (Lower left) Workshop company retrieving a Russian Tank. ● (Upper left) Men of the 1st Platoon of the 1st Panzer Division removing Kübel engine. ● (Right) Factory yard filled with 7.5-cm. antitank guns.

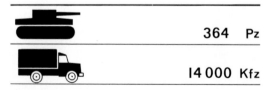

364 Pz

14 000 Kfz

Repair production for 1st Panzer Army Jan. 1, 1942 - March 31, 1942. 364 Panzers, 14,000 vehicles.

Here Stalin Won More than a Battle

"Obstacles for bravery and boldness do not exist -forward soldiers to heroism"! were the slogans on the signs which bordered the smashed roads to the Crimea, after the Soviets gained the first bridgehead at Sivash during the winter of 1943 (Upper right). Tolbukhins' Armies stormed the peninsula at this place on April 7, 1944, and four weeks later raised their flag on a bulwark in Sevastopol. ● (Lower left) Army General Tolbukhin on the right with Marshal Vasilevski (Left) at his battle command post. ● (Upper left) Liwadia Palace in Yalta where the Crimean conference between Roosevelt, Churchill and Stalin took place February 1945. Division of the world, and the fate of Germany was sealed. (*Scorched Earth*, pages 408-418).

Disastrous Crimea
(Above) Soviet photo titled: "Remains of the German Crimea Army." They were not the remains, but the very last, holding a port which no ship touched anymore — the last of the 111th I.D. or the 50th I.D., from the 336th, the 73rd or the 98th, impossible to document. They remained on the ill-fated island. ● The escaped survivors of the hellish Crimea thanked god when they arrived in the harbor of Konstanza (Right).
Scorched Earth, pages 421-425).

416/417

Dark Signs of Revenge and Retaliation
46th I.D. evacuated Feodosia in December 1941, leaving behind all their gravely wounded. Those left behind alive were found dead, half covered by the ruins of an embankment wall when the 105th Infantry Regiment retook the city on January 18, 1942. They were either beaten to death or thrown off the wall.

The Barbaric Gallows of Voronezh.
A female partisan condemned to death by the execution commandand hung from a statue of Lenin. Intended as a deterrent, this form of enforcement showed a surprising cruelty. No wonder it turned into a deep hatred by the population.

Execution at Kodyma.
A secret photo taken by "soldier H." through the bent arm of the man in front of him. One hundred partisans were shot. Four hundred drifted into the town of Kodyma, region of Nikolajev, to liquidate the headquarters of a German Infantry Division. They were betrayed, caught and everyone carrying a weapon, shot. The massacre took place in the twilight; in the blurred focus the reflections of the muzzle flashes on the backs of the victims present a ghostly, unreal picture.

(Above) Panorama of Vitebsk on the Dvina. ● Dvina bridge. ● Bridge over the Vitba. ● Main-street, the Maria Assumption Cathedral. (Lower row) Nevel the city on the road from Vitebsk to Lake Ilmen.

Russen
Kessel

OSTSEE

Reval

Peipus-See

Frontverlauf am
28.7.1944

Frontverlauf am
22.6 1944

N

Riga

Dünaburg

Newel

Düna

Witebsk

Autobahn-Moskau

Smolensk

Memel

Königsberg

Wilna

OST-PREUSSEN

Danzig

Suwalki

Njemen

Minsk

Beresina

Mogilew

Dnjepr

Baranowitschi

Bobruisk

Weichsel

Warschau

Bug

Pripjet

Brest-Litowsk

Sümpfe

Pripjet

Baranow

Kowel

0 50 100 200
km

Rowno

Kiew

Schitomir

The Helmet on the Wagon Wheel
How many times did the bakers, tailors and shoe-makers grab their helmets and help to stop the enemy from breaking through. The question: "Buddy, could you fix this in a hurry" turned into bloody reality. ● (Right) 10,000 loaves of bread were baked daily in the ovens of a bakery company.

This Was the Railroad Station at Smolensk
Countless German soldiers used this junction, to the Eastern Front. The city was given up September 24, 1943. The station, including the entire track installations were blown up by combat engineers.

	Jahre	PFERDE UND MAULESELBESTAND DER WEHRMACHT	= 500 000
KRIEGSEINTRITT	1939		573 000
EINGESETZT INSGESAMT	1941 1945		2.75 Millo.
EINGESETZT IN RUSSLAND	1941 1945		2.07 Millo.
VERLUSTE INSGESAMT BIS KRIEGSENDE	1941 1945		1.7 Millo.

Tanks Versus Horses

Occurring June 3, 1944 south-west of Vitebsk. A Russian armored scout group broke through and shot the horse-drawn hospital of the 6th Corps to pieces. ● Tanks against horses! Thinking of the war in Russia one imagines only tanks — but horses were its manifestation. More than two million were used by the Germans. Making their way with the Army through the endless country, despite mud, snow or dust. Their work and their misery is well worth a memorial.

The Battle Group
The indelible image of defensive combat. 5th SS-Panzer Division *Wiking* confronted the Soviet onslaught at Kovel. Getting ready for a counter attack is the 12th Company of the *Germania* Regiment.

Summer Battle of the Center Sector
The Russians are coming. The great assault begins.
Don't worry about rank, uniform or shoulder straps:
man and his weapon, nothing else counts. ● (Left) At
the eye-piece. ● (Above) Heavy Infantry gun is loaded. ●
"Fire"!

The Front Caves In
During the miserable retreat, bordering on flight the photographer found a gesture of humanity (Left). ● Soviet Infantry Regiments fighting for Polotsk, situated on the right wing of Army Group Center; a "Fortified" place held by parts of the 16th Army. (*Scorched Earth*, page 433).

Comrades
(Left) Forty shell fragments hit the platoon leader of the 26th I.D. (Above)
Men of the Division *Feldherrnhalle* at Narva rescue their orderly. (Below) In
the cauldron of Minsk: "You got a connection"?

432/433

The Soviets Broke Through
Russian 416th Division on their way westward
(Upper left). ● (Lower left) Caught in the debacle of
Army Group Center, thousands of Landser disguised
as civilians, reached East Prussia after weeks of
marching. The official term: "Rückkämpfer"
(Those who fought their way back). ● (Upper right)
Intervening reserves tried in vain to check the Soviet
advance to the Vistula. Resisting for a few hours,
then back a couple kilometers. Make another stand
and move back — again and again. For days. For
weeks. ● The men fell dead-tired into the ditches
during a short rest.

Soldiers of 1944

Top row: Old veterans of the Eastern Front, privates and PFC's, initiate with the handling of a Panzerfaust and the cunning of man-to-man fighting, and all of the other problems of survival. Below: Juvenile faces appeared on the front. They questioned the veterans: "Tell me . . ." or "What hit you there"? ● Lower right: Even the Russians were recruiting. ● Partisans of the liberated regions are inducted into the Red Army.

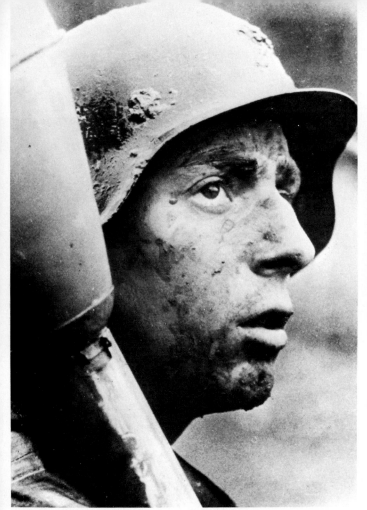

On East Prussia's Borders

The battle for the Reich begins

Appendix

The Insignias of the German Divisions

Infanteriedivisionen

1. Infanteriedivision
Wehrkreis I Königsberg
Grenadierregiment 1 und 43
Füsilierregiment 22
Artillerieregiment 1

14. Infanteriedivision (mot.)
Wehrkreis IV Dresden
Grenadierregiment
11 und 53
Artillerieregiment 14

6. Infanteriedivision
Wehrkreis VI Münster
Grenadierregiment
18, 37 und 58
Artillerieregiment 6

15. Infanteriedivision
Wehrkreis IX Kassel
Grenadierregiment
81, 88 und 106
Artillerieregiment 15

7. Infanteriedivision
Wehrkreis VII München
Grenadierregiment
19, 61 und 62
Artillerieregiment 7

17. Infanteriedivision
Wehrkreis XIII Nürnberg
Grenadierregiment
21, 55 und 95
Artillerieregiment 17

9. Infanteriedivision
Wehrkreis IX Kassel
Grenadierregiment
36, 57 und 116
Artillerieregiment 9

21. Infanteriedivision
Wehrkreis I Königsberg
Grenadierregiment
3, 24 und 45
Artillerieregiment 21

11. Infanteriedivision
Wehrkreis I Königsberg
Grenadierregiment
2, 23 und 44
Artillerieregiment 11

22. Infanteriedivision
Wehrkreis X Hamburg
Grenadierregiment
16, 47 und 65
Artillerieregiment 22

12. Infanteriedivision
Wehrkreis II Stettin
Füsilierregiment 27
Grenadierregiment 48 und 89
Artillerieregiment 12

23. Infanteriedivision
Wehrkreis III Berlin
Grenadierregiment 9 und 67
Füsilierregiment 68
Artillerieregiment 23

24. Infanteriedivision
Wehrkreis IV Dresden
Grenadierregiment
31, 32 und 102
Artillerieregiment 24

36. Infanteriedivision (mot.)
Wehrkreis XII Wiesbaden
Grenadierregiment
70, 87 und 118
Artillerieregiment 36

26. Infanteriedivision
Wehrkreis VI Münster
Grenadierregiment
39, 77 und 78
Artillerieregiment 26

**Reichsgrenadierdivision
›Hoch- und Deutschmeister‹**
Wehrkreis XVII Wien
Grenadierregiment 131, 132
u. 134, Artillerieregiment 96

30. Infanteriedivision
Wehrkreis X Hamburg
Grenadierregiment 6 und 46
Füsilierregiment 26
Artillerieregiment 30

45. Infanteriedivision
Wehrkreis XVII Wien
Grenadierregiment
130, 133 und 135
Artillerieregiment 98

31. Infanteriedivision
Wehrkreis XI Hannover
Grenadierregiment
12, 17 und 82
Artillerieregiment 31

46. Infanteriedivision
Wehrkreis XIII Nürnberg
Grenadierregiment
42, 72 und 97
Artillerieregiment 114

32. Infanteriedivision
Wehrkreis II Stettin
Grenadierregiment
4, 94 und 96
Artillerieregiment 32

50. Infanteriedivision
Wehrkreis III Berlin
Grenadierregiment
121, 122 und 123
Artillerieregiment 150

34. Infanteriedivision
Wehrkreis XII Wiesbaden
Grenadierregiment
80, 107 und 253
Artillerieregiment 34

52. Infanteriedivision
Wehrkreis IX Kassel
Grenadierregiment
163, 181 und 205
Artillerieregiment 152

35. Infanteriedivision
Wehrkreis V Stuttgart
Grenadierregiment 109, 111
Füsilierregiment 34
Artillerieregiment 35

56. Infanteriedivision
Wehrkreis IV Dresden
Grenadierregiment
171, 192 und 234
Artillerieregiment 156

57. Infanteriedivision
Wehrkreis VII München
Grenadierregiment
179, 199 und 217
Artillerieregiment 157

58. Infanteriedivision
Wehrkreis X Hamburg
Grenadierregiment
154, 209 und 220
Artillerieregiment 158

61. Infanteriedivision
Wehrkreis I Königsberg
Grenadierregiment
151, 162 und 176
Artillerieregiment 161

62. Infanteriedivision
Wehrkreis VIII Breslau
Grenadierregiment
164, 183 und 190
Artillerieregiment 162

65. Infanteriedivision
Wehrkreis XII Wiesbaden
Grenadierregiment
145, 146 und 147
Artillerieregiment 165

68. Infanteriedivision
Wehrkreis III Berlin
Grenadierregiment
169, 188 und 196
Artillerieregiment 168

71. Infanteriedivision
Wehrkreis XI Hannover
Grenadierregiment
191, 194 und 211
Artillerieregiment 171

72. Infanteriedivision
Wehrkreis XII Wiesbaden
Grenadierregiment
105, 124 und 266
Artillerieregiment 172

73. Infanteriedivision
Wehrkreis XIII Nürnberg
Grenadierregiment
170, 186 und 213
Artillerieregiment 173

75. Infanteriedivision
Wehrkreis II Stettin
Grenadierregiment 172, 222
Füsilierregiment 202
Artillerieregiment 175

76. Infanteriedivision
Wehrkreis III Berlin
Grenadierregiment 178, 203
Füsilierregiment 230
Artillerieregiment 176

78. Sturmdivision
Wehrkeis V Stuttgart
Sturmregiment
14, 195 und 215
Artillerieregiment 178

79. Infanteriedivision
Wehrkreis XII Wiesbaden
Grenadierregiment
208, 212 und 226
Artillerieregiment 179

81. Infanteriedivision
Wehrkreis VIII Breslau
Grenadierregiment
161, 174 und 189
Artillerieregiment 181

83. Infanteriedivision
Wehrkreis X Hamburg
Grenadierregiment
251, 257 und 277
Artillerieregiment 183

86. Infanteriedivision
Wehrkreis VI Münster
Grenadierregiment
167, 184 und 216
Artillerieregiment 186

87. Infanteriedivision
Wehrkreis IV Dresden
Grenadierregiment
173, 185 und 187
Artillerieregiment 187

88. Infanteriedivision
Wehrkreis XIII Nürnberg
Grenadierregiment
245, 246 und 248
Artillerieregiment 188

93. Infanteriedivision
Wehrkreis III Berlin
Grenadierregiment
270, 271 und 272
Artillerieregiment 193

94. Infanteriedivision
Wehrkreis IV Dresden
Grenadierregiment
267, 274 und 276
Artillerieregiment 194

95. Infanteriedivision
Wehrkreis IX Kassel
Grenadierregiment
278, 279 und 280
Artillerieregiment 195

96. Infanteriedivision
Wehrkreis XI Hannover
Grenadierregiment
283, 284 und 287
Artillerieregiment 196

98. Infanteriedivision
Wehrkreis XIII Nürnberg
Grenadierregiment
117, 289 und 290
Artillerieregiment 198

102. Infanteriedivision
Wehrkreis VIII Breslau
Grenadierregiment
84, 232 und 233
Artillerieregiment 104

106. Infanteriedivision
Wehrkreis VI Münster
Grenadierregiment
239, 240 und 241
Artillerieregiment 107

110. Infanteriedivision
Wehrkreis X Hamburg
Grenadierregiment
252, 254 und 255
Artillerieregiment 120

111. Infanteriedivision
Wehrkreis XI Hannover
Grenadierregiment
50, 70 und 117
Artillerieregiment 117

112. Infanteriedivision
Wehrkreis XII Wiesbaden
Grenadierregiment
110, 256 und 258
Artillerieregiment 86

121. Infanteriedivision
Wehrkreis I Königsberg
Grenadierregiment
405, 407 und 408
Artillerieregiment 121

122. Infanteriedivision
Wehrkreis II Stettin
Grenadierregiment
409, 410 und 411
Artillerieregiment 122

125. Infanteriedivision
Wehrkreis V Stuttgart
Grenadierregiment
419, 420 und 421
Artillerieregiment 125

126. Infanteriedivision
Wehrkreis VI Münster
Grenadierregiment
422, 424 und 426
Artillerieregiment 126

129. Infanteriedivision
Wehrkreis IX Kassel
Grenadierregiment
427, 428 und 430
Artillerieregiment 129

131. Infanteriedivision
Wehrkreis XI Hannover
Grenadierregiment
431, 432 und 434
Artillerieregiment 131

132. Infanteriedivision
Wehrkreis XII Wiesbaden
Grenadierregiment
436, 437 und 438
Artillerieregiment 132

134. Infanteriedivision
Wehrkreis IV Dresden
Grenadierregiment
439, 445 und 446
Artillerieregiment 134

137. Infanteriedivision
Wehrkreis XVII Wien
Grenadierregiment
447, 448 und 449
Artillerieregiment 137

161. Infanteriedivision
Wehrkreis I Königsberg
Grenadierregiment
336, 364 und 371
Artillerieregiment 241

164. Infanteriedivision
Wehrkreis IV Dresden
Grenadierregiment
382, 433 und 440
Artillerieregiment 220

167. Infanteriedivision
Wehrkreis VII München
Grenadierregiment 315,
331 und 339
Artillerieregiment 238

168. Infanteriedivision
Wehrkreis VIII Breslau
Grenadierregiment
417, 429 und 442
Artillerieregiment 248

169. Infanteriedivision
Wehrkreis IX Kassel
Grenadierregiment
378, 379 und 392
Artillerieregiment 230

170. Infanteriedivision
Wehrkreis X Hamburg
Grenadierregiment
391, 399 und 401
Artillerieregiment 240

197. Infanteriedivision
Wehrkreis XII Wiesbaden
Grenadierregiment
321, 332 und 347
Artillerieregiment 229

198. Infanteriedivision
Wehrkreis V Stuttgart
Grenadierregiment
305, 308 und 326
Artillerieregiment 235

205. Infanteriedivision
Wehrkreis V Stuttgart
Grenadierregiment
335, 353 und 358
Artillerieregiment 205

206. Infanteriedivision
Wehrkreis I Königsberg
Grenadierregiment
301, 312 und 413
Artillerieregiment 206

207. Infanteriedivision
Wehrkreis II Stettin
Infanterieregiment
322, 368 und 374
Artillerieregiment 207

208. Infanteriedivision
Wehrkreis III Berlin
Grenadierregiment
309, 337 und 338
Artillerieregiment 208

215. Infanteriedivision
Wehrkreis V Stuttgart
Grenadierregiment
380, 390 und 435
Artillerieregiment 215

216. Infanteriedivision
Wehrkreis XI Hannover
Grenadierregiment
348, 396 und 398
Artillerieregiment 216

217. Infanteriedivision
Wehrkreis I Königsberg
Grenadierregiment
311, 346 und 389
Artillerieregiment 217

218. Infanteriedivision
Wehrkreis III Berlin
Grenadierregiment
323, 386 und 397
Artillerieregiment 218

223. Infanteriedivision
Wehrkreis IV Dresden
Grenadierregiment
344, 385 und 425
Artillerieregiment 223

225. Infanteriedivision
Wehrkreis X Hamburg
Grenadierregiment
333, 376 und 377
Artillerieregiment 225

227. Infanteriedivision
Wehrkreis VI Münster
Grenadierregiment
328, 366 und 412
Artillerieregiment 227

250. Infanteriedivision span.
Wehrkreis XIII Nürnberg
Grenadierregiment
262, 263 und 269
Artillerieregiment 250

258. Infanteriedivision
Wehrkreis II Stettin
Grenadierregiment
458, 478 und 479
Artillerieregiment 258

251. Infanteriedivision
Wehrkreis IX Kassel
Grenadierregiment
451, 459 und 471
Artillerieregiment 251

260. Infanteriedivision
Wehrkreis V Stuttgart
Grenadierregiment
460, 470 und 480
Artillerieregiment 260

252. Infanteriedivision
Wehrkreis VIII Breslau
Grenadierregiment
7, 461 und 472
Artillerieregiment 252

262. Infanteriedivision
Wehrkreis XVII Wien
Grenadierregiment
462, 482 und 486
Artillerieregiment 262

253. Infanteriedivision
Wehrkreis VI Münster
Grenadierregiment
453, 464 und 473
Artillerieregiment 253

263. Infanteriedivision
Wehrkreis XII Wiesbaden
Grenadierregiment
463, 483 und 485
Artillerieregiment 263

255. Infanteriedivision
Wehrkreis IV Dresden
Grenadierregiment
455, 465 und 475
Artillerieregiment 255

267. Infanteriedivision
Wehrkreis XI Hannover
Grenadierregiment
467, 487 und 497
Artillerieregiment 267

256. Infanteriedivision
Wehrkreis IV Dresden
Grenadierregiment
456, 476 und 481
Artillerieregiment 256

268. Infanteriedivision
Wehrkreis VII München
Grenadierregiment
468, 488 und 499
Artillerieregiment 268

257. Infanteriedivision
Wehrkreis III Berlin
Grenadierregiment
457, 466 und 477
Artillerieregiment 257

269. Infanteriedivision
Wehrkreis X Hamburg
Grenadierregiment
469, 489 und 490
Artillerieregiment 269

272. Infanteriedivision
Wehrkreis XI Hannover
Grenadierregiment
980, 981 und 982
Artillerieregiment 272

278. Infanteriedivision
Wehrkreis III Berlin
Grenadierregiment
992, 993 und 994
Artillerieregiment 278

282. Infanteriedivision
Wehrkreis V Stuttgart
Grenadierregiment
848, 849 und 850
Artillerieregiment 282

290. Infanteriedivision
Wehrkreis X Hamburg
Grenadierregiment
501, 502 und 503
Artillerieregiment 290

291. Infanteriedivision
Wehrkreis I Königsberg
Grenadierregiment
504, 505 und 506
Artillerieregiment 291

292. Infanteriedivision
Wehrkreis II Stettin
Grenadierregiment
507, 508 und 509
Artillerieregiment 292

294. Infanteriedivision
Wehrkreis IV Dresden
Grenadierregiment
513, 514 und 515
Artillerieregiment 294

296. Infanteriedivision
Wehrkreis XIII Nürnberg
Grenadierregiment
519, 520 und 521
Artillerieregiment 296

299. Infanteriedivision
Wehrkreis IX Kassel
Grenadierregiment
528, 529 und 530
Artillerieregiment 299

302. Infanteriedivision
Wehrkreis II Stettin
Grenadierregiment
570, 571 und 572
Artillerieregiment 302

305. Infanteriedivision
Wehrkreis V Stuttgart
Grenadierregiment
576, 577 und 578
Artillerieregiment 305

306. Infanteriedivision
Wehrkreis VI Münster
Grenadierregiment
579, 580 und 581
Artillerieregiment 306

320. Infanteriedivision
Wehrkreis X Hamburg
Grenadierregiment
585, 586 und 587
Artillerieregiment 320

323. Infanteriedivision
Wehrkreis V Stuttgart
Grenadierregiment
591, 593 und 594
Artillerieregiment 323

329. Infanteriedivision
Wehrkreis VI Münster
Grenadierregiment
551, 552 und 553
Artillerieregiment 329

331. Infanteriedivision
Wehrkreis XVII Wien
Grenadierregiment
557, 558 und 559
Artillerieregiment 331

335. Infanteriedivision
Wehrkreis V Stuttgart
Grenadierregiment
682, 683 und 684
Artillerieregiment 335

336. Infanteriedivision
Wehrkreis IV Dresden
Grenadierregiment
685, 686 und 687
Artillerieregiment 336

357. Infanteriedivision
Wehrkreis IV Dresden
Grenadierregiment
944, 945 und 946
Artillerieregiment 357

362. Infanteriedivision
Wehrkreis VII München
Grenadierregiment
954, 955 und 956
Artillerieregiment 362

369. Infanteriedivision
Wehrkreis XVII Wien
Grenadierregiment
369 und 370
Artillerieregiment 369

373. Infanteriedivision
Wehrkreis XVII Wien
Grenadierregiment
383 und 384
Artillerieregiment 373

376. Infanteriedivision
Wehrkreis VII München
Grenadierregiment
672, 673 und 767
Artillerieregiment 376

384. Infanteriedivision
Wehrkreis IV Dresden
Grenadierregiment
534, 535 und 536
Artillerieregiment 384

392. Infanteriedivision
Wehrkreis XVII Wien
Grenadierregiment
846 und 847
Artillerieregiment 392

707. Infanteriedivision
Wehrkreis VII München
Grenadierregiment 727 und
747
Artillerieabteilung 657

715. Infanteriedivision
Wehrkreis V Stuttgart
Grenadierregiment
725, 735 und 1028
Artillerieregiment 671

Jägerdivisionen

5. Jägerdivision
Wehrkreis V Stuttgart
Jägerregiment
56 und 75
Artillerieregiment 5

97. Jägerdivision
Wehrkreis VII München
Jägerregiment
204 und 207
Artillerieregiment 81

8. Jägerdivision
Wehrkreis VIII Breslau
Jägerregiment
28 und 38
Artillerieregiment 8

100. Jägerdivision
Wehrkreis XVII Wien
Jägerregiment
54, 227 und 369
Artillerieregiment 83

28. Jägerdivision
Wehrkreis VIII Breslau
Jägerregiment
49 und 83
Artillerieregiment 28

101. Jägerdivision
Wehrkreis V Stuttgart
Jägerregiment
228 und 229
Artillerieregiment 85

Gebirgsdivisionen

1. Gebirgsdivision
Wehrkreis VII München
Gebirgsjägerregiment
98 und 99
Gebirgsartillerieregiment 79

4. Gebirgsdivision
Wehrkreis V/VIII Stuttg. Bresl.
Gebirgsjägerregiment
13 und 91
Gebirgsartillerieregiment 94

2. Gebirgsdivision
Wehrkreis XVIII Salzburg
Gebirgsjägerregiment
136 und 137
Gebirgsartillerieregiment 111

5. Gebirgsdivision
Wehrkreis VII/XIII/XVIII
München, Nürnberg, Salzburg
Gebirgsjägerregiment 85, 100
Gebirgsartillerieregiment 95

3. Gebirgsdivision
Wehrkreis XVIII Salzburg
Gebirgsjägerregiment
138 und 144
Gebirgsartillerieregiment 112

6. Gebirgsdivision
Wehrkreis XVIII Salzburg
Gebirgsjägerregiment
141 und 143
Gebirgsartillerieregiment 118

7. Gebirgsdivision
Wehrkreis XIII Nürnberg
Gebirgsjägerregiment
206 und 218
Gebirgsartillerieregiment 82

10. Gebirgsdivision
Wehrkreis XVIII Salzburg
Gebirgsjägerregiment 139
Jägerbataillon 3 und 6
Gebirgsartillerieregiment 931

Luftwaffenfelddivisionen

13. Luftwaffenfelddivision
Wehrkreis III Stettin
Jägerregiment Luftwaffe
25 und 26
Artillerieregiment 13

21. Luftwaffenfelddivision
Wehrkreis III Stettin
Jägerregiment Luftwaffe
41, 42 und 43
Artillerieregiment 21

Panzergrenadierdivisionen

3. Panzergrenadierdivision
Wehrkreis III Berlin
Gren.-Regiment (mot.) 8, 28
Panzerabteilung 103
Artillerieregiment 3

20. Panzergrenadierdivision
Wehrkreis X Hamburg
Gren.-Regiment (mot.) 76, 90
Panzerabteilung 8
Artillerieregiment 20

10. Panzergrenadierdivision
Wehrkreis XIII Nürnberg
Gren.-Regiment (mot.) 20, 41
Panzerabteilung 7
Artillerieregiment 10

25. Panzergrenadierdivision
Wehrkreis V Stuttgart
Gren.-Regiment (mot.) 35, 119
Panzerabteilung 5
Artillerieregiment 25

16. Panzergrenadierdivision
Wehrkreis VI Münster
Gren.-Regiment (mot.) 60, 156
Panzerabteilung 116
Artillerieregiment 146

29. Panzergrenadierdivision
Wehrkreis IX Kassel
Gren.-Regiment (mot.) 15, 71
Panzerabteilung 129
Artillerieregiment 29

18. Panzergrenadierdivision
Wehrkreis VIII Breslau
Gren.-Regiment (mot.) 30, 51
Panzerabteilung 118
Artillerieregiment 18

60. Panzergrenadierdivision
Wehrkreis XX Danzig
Gren.-Regiment (mot.) 92, 120
Panzerabteilung 160
Artillerieregiment 160

**Panzergrenadierdivision
Feldherrnhalle**
Wehrkreis XX Danzig
Grenadierregiment FHH
Füsilierregiment FHH
Panzerabteilung FHH
Artillerieregiment FHH

**Panzergrenadierdivision
Großdeutschland**
Wehrkreis III Berlin
Panzergrenadierregiment GD
Panzerfüsilierregiment GD
Panzerregiment GD
Artillerieregiment GD

Panzerdivisionen

1. Panzerdivision
Wehrkreis IX Kassel
Pz.-Grenadierregiment 1, 113
Panzerregiment 1
Pz.-Artillerieregiment 73

6. Panzerdivision
Wehrkreis VI Münster
Pz.-Grenadierregiment 4, 114
Panzerregiment 11
Pz.-Artillerieregiment 76

2. Panzerdivision
Wehrkreis XVII Wien
Pz.-Grenadierregiment 2, 304
Panzerregiment 3
Pz.-Artillerieregiment 74

7. Panzerdivision
Wehrkreis IX Kassel
Pz.-Grenadierregiment 6, 7
Panzerregiment 25
Pz.-Artillerieregiment 78

3. Panzerdivision
Wehrkreis III Berlin
Pz.-Grenadierregiment 3, 394
Panzerregiment 6
Pz.-Artillerieregiment 75

8. Panzerdivision
Wehrkreis III Berlin
Pz.-Grenadierregiment 8, 28
Panzerregiment 10
Pz.-Artillerieregiment 80

4. Panzerdivision
Wehrkreis XIII Nürnberg
Pz.-Grenadierregiment 12, 33
Panzerregiment 35
Pz.-Artillerieregiment 103

9. Panzerdivision
Wehrkreis XVII Wien
Pz.-Grenadierregiment 10, 11
Panzerregiment 33
Pz.-Artillerieregiment 102

5. Panzerdivision
Wehrkreis VIII Breslau
Pz.-Grenadierregiment 13, 14
Panzerregiment 31
Pz.-Artillerieregiment 116

10. Panzerdivision
Wehrkreis V Stuttgart
Pz.-Grenadierregiment 69, 86
Panzerregiment 7
Pz.-Artillerieregiment 90

11. Panzerdivision
Wehrkreis VIII Breslau
Pz.-Gren.-Regiment 110, 111
Panzerregiment 15
Pz.-Artillerieregiment 119

19. Panzerdivision
Wehrkreis XI Hannover
Pz.-Grenadierregiment 73, 74
Panzerregiment 27
Pz.-Artillerieregiment 19

12. Panzerdivision
Wehrkreis II Stettin
Pz.-Grenadierregiment 5, 25
Panzerregiment 29
Pz.-Artillerieregiment 2

20. Panzerdivision
Wehrkr. IX Kassel XI Hann.
Pz.-Grenadierregiment 59, 112
Panzerregiment 21
Pz.-Artillerieregiment 92

13. Panzerdivision
Wehrkreis XI Hannover
Pz.-Grenadierregiment 66, 93
Panzerregiment 4
Pz.-Artillerieregiment 13

21. Panzerdivision
Wehrkreis VI Münster
Pz.-Gren.-Regiment 125, 192
Panzerregiment 100 (22)
Pz.-Artillerieregiment 155

14. Panzerdivision
Wehrkreis IV Dresden
Pz.-Gren.-Regiment 103, 108
Panzerregiment 36
Pz.-Artillerieregiment 4

22. Panzerdivision
Wehrkreis XII Wiesbaden
Pz.-Gren.-Regiment 129, 140
Panzerregiment 204
Pz.-Artillerieregiment 140

16. Panzerdivision
Wehrkreis VI Münster
Pz.-Grenadierregiment 64, 79
Panzerregiment 2
Pz.-Artillerieregiment 16

23. Panzerdivision
Wehrkreis V Stuttgart
Pz.-Gren.-Regiment 126, 128
Panzerregiment 23
Pz.-Artillerieregiment 128

17. Panzerdivision
Wehrkreis VII München
Pz.-Grenadierregiment 40, 63
Panzerregiment 39
Pz.-Artillerieregiment 27

24. Panzerdivision
Wehrkreis I Königsberg
Pz.-Grenadierregiment 21, 26
Panzerregiment 24
Pz.-Artillerieregiment 89

18. Panzerdivision
Wehrkreis IV Dresden
Pz.-Grenadierregiment 52, 101
Panzerregiment 18
Pz.-Artillerieregiment 88

Vor Umstellung:
1. Kavalleriedivision
Reiterregiment 1, 2 und 22
Kavallerieregiment 21
r. Artillerieregiment 1

25. Panzerdivision
Wehrkreis VI Münster
Pz.-Gren.-Regiment 146, 147
Panzerregiment 9
Pz.-Artillerieregiment 91

116. Panzerdivision
Wehrkreis VI Münster
Pz.-Gren.-Regiment 60, 156
Panzerregiment 16
Pz.-Artillerieregiment 146

26. Panzerdivision
Wehrkreis III Berlin
Pz.-Gren.-Regiment 9, 67
Panzerregiment 26
Pz.-Artillerieregiment 93

Divisionen der Waffen-SS

1. SS.-Panzerdivision
Leibstandarte Adolf Hitler
SS-Pz.-Gren.-Regiment 1 u. 2
SS-Panzerregiment 1
SS-Pz.-Artillerieregiment 1

5. SS-Panzerdivision
Wiking
SS-Pz.-Gren.-Regim. 9 u. 10
SS-Panzerregiment 5
SS-Pz.-Artillerieregiment 5

2. SS-Panzerdivision
Das Reich
SS-Pz.-Gren.-Regiment 3 u. 4
SS-Panzerregiment 2
SS-Pz.-Artillerieregiment 2

9. SS-Panzerdivision
Hohenstaufen
SS-Pz.-Gren.-Regim. 19 u. 20
SS-Panzerregiment 9
SS-Pz.-Artillerieregiment 9

3. SS-Panzerdivision
Totenkopf
SS-Pz.-Gren.-Regiment 5 u. 6
SS-Panzerregiment 3
SS-Pz.-Artillerieregiment 3

10. SS-Panzerdivision
Frundsberg
SS.-Pz.-Gren.-Reg. 21 u. 22
SS-Panzerregiment 10
SS-Pz.-Artillerieregiment 10

4. SS-Polizei
Panzergrenadierdivision
Pol.-Pz.-Gren.-Regim. 7. u. 8
SS-Panzerabteilung 4
SS-Pz.-Artillerieregiment 4

11. SS-Panzergrenadierdiv.
Nordland
SS-Pz.-Gren.-Regim. 23 u. 24
SS-Panzerabteilung 11
SS-Pz.-Artillerieregiment 11

16. Pz.-Grenadierdivision
Reichsführer SS
SS-Pz.-Gren.-Regim. 35 u. 36
SS-Panzerabteilung 16
SS-Pz.-Artillerieregiment 16

23. SS-Gebirgsdivision
Kama
SS-Geb.-Jägerregiment 55, 56
SS-Gebirgsartillerie 23

17. SS-Panzergrenadierdiv.
Götz von Berlichingen
SS-Pz.-Gren-Regim. 37 u. 38
SS-Panzerabteilung 17
SS-Pz.-Artillerieregiment 17

28. SS-Panzergrenadierdiv.
Wallonien
SS-Pz.-Gren.-Regim. 69,
70 und 71
SS-Panzerabteilung 28
SS-Pz.-Artillerieregiment 28

18. SS-Panzergrenadierdiv.
Horst Wessel
SS-Pz.-Gren.-Regim. 39. u. 40
SS-Panzerabteilung 18
SS-Pz.-Artillerieregiment 18

38. SS-Panzergrenadierdiv.
Nibelungen
SS-Pz.-Gren.-Regim. 95,
96 und 97
SS-Panzerabteilung 38
SS-Pz.-Artillerieregiment 38

Sturmgeschützbrigaden

184. Sturmgeschützbrigade
aufgestellt Spätersommer
1940 in Zinna bei
Jüterbog

197. Sturmgeschützbrigade
aufgestellt Winter
1940/41 in Jüterbog

189. Sturmgeschützabteilung
aufgestellt 9. Juli 1941

237. Sturmgeschützbrigade
aufgestellt im Sommer
1943 in Posen

190. Sturmgeschützbrigade
aufgestellt 1. Oktober
1940 in Jüterbog

259. Sturmgeschützbrigade
aufgestellt Juni
1943 in Jüterbog

279. Sturmgeschützbrigade
aufgestellt am 1. 7. 1943
in Neiße

 **Sturmgeschützbrigade
Großdeutschland**
aufgestellt Sommer 1940

 666. Sturmgeschützbatterie
aufgestellt Mitte Mai
1940 in Zinna

Photo Acknowledgements

Adam, Herbert(1), Andres, Erich (3), Archiv (53), Associated Press (3), Bäke, Dr. Franz (1), Bange, Josef (1), Bauer, Erich (4), Brämer, Hans (1) Brütting, Georg (14), Burg, *Oberleutnant* (5), Cusian, Albert (8), Determeyer, Prof. C. (3), Dethleffsen, Christian (1), Dornhofer, Hans (1), Felde, Andres (3) Franz, Gerhard (1), Gebauer, Ernst (1), Hackl, Walter (16), Heinrich, Carl (45), Heysing, Günther (49), Holters(13), Hubmann, Hanns (4), Imperial War Museum, London (26), Jakatzki, Franz (1), Jollasse, Erwin (1), Kandutsch, Hermann (5), Klippert, Hanns-Ritter (4), Klöckner, Hans (8), Knödler, Karl (16), Krüger, Hans (1), Kuntz, Herbert (3), Lahs, Rolf (1), Moll, Jakob (Member of the former 39th) (3), Musculus, Friedrich (1), Niederlein, Fritz G. (7), Novosti Agency, Moscow (66), Oster-reichischer Organization of the 139th Geberigsjägerregiment (3), Ott, Dr. Alfred (33), Hilmar, Pabel (1), Paulus, Ernst A. (29), Pläsker, Willi (1), Pein, Klaus (2), Priesack, Prof. Dr. (1), Regnery, Franz (1), Remmer, Asmus (4), Renz, Dr. Manfred (1), Rust, Paul (1), Salchow, Gerhard (4), Saint-Loup (4), Salié, Adolf (1), Scheibert, Horst (5), Schmidt, Dr. Hermann (7), Schöttl, Dr. Oskar (1), Schubert, Hans (1), Schürer, Hans (18), Schwabe, Alfred (6), Schwoon, Karl (8), Seelbach, Walter (4), Sellhorn, Heinz (4), Sparr, Adolf (1), Steen, Ernst (1), von Steinkeller, Friedrich-Karl (1), Stöcker, Paul (23), Stoves, Rolf (9), Strippel, Hans (1), Tenning, Otto (3), Thien, Günther (2), Thoss, Dr. Alfred (1), Thrän, Emil (19), Tietz, Gerhard (23), Tornau, Gottfried (2), Tripp, Hans-Joachim (9), Trischler, Alfred (12), Türk, Dr. Hermann (7), Ullstein Archives (48), Westphal, Werner (2), Winterfeld, Dr. Kurt (5).

The photographs on pages 320/321 and 342/243 are with kind permission from the book, *Soldat in der Telegraphen und Nachrichtentruppe*, Selbstverlag, Würzburg 1965, by Albert Praun.

Divisional Insignias by Michael Prügel

About the author:

Paul Carell was born in Thuringia in 1911, studied political economy, philosophy and psychology, and received his doctorate of philosophy in 1936. In the foreign service until the war began, he has worked as a journalist and writer since the war. His books have been translated into twelve languages.
Paul Carell lives in Hamburg.

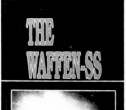